Spiritual Answers
to Guide Your Life

WENDY EDWARDS

BALBOA
PRESS
A DIVISION OF HAY HOUSE

Copyright © 2011 Wendy Edwards.

All rights reserved. No part of this book may be used or reproduced by any means, graphic, electronic, or mechanical, including photocopying, recording, taping or by any information storage retrieval system without the written permission of the publisher except in the case of brief quotations embodied in critical articles and reviews.

Balboa Press books may be ordered through booksellers or by contacting:

Balboa Press
A Division of Hay House
1663 Liberty Drive
Bloomington, IN 47403
www.balboapress.com
1-(877) 407-4847

Because of the dynamic nature of the Internet, any web addresses or links contained in this book may have changed since publication and may no longer be valid. The views expressed in this work are solely those of the author and do not necessarily reflect the views of the publisher, and the publisher hereby disclaims any responsibility for them.

The author of this book does not dispense medical advice or prescribe the use of any technique as a form of treatment for physical, emotional, or medical problems without the advice of a physician, either directly or indirectly. The intent of the author is only to offer information of a general nature to help you in your quest for emotional and spiritual well-being. In the event you use any of the information in this book for yourself, which is your constitutional right, the author and the publisher assume no responsibility for your actions.

Any people depicted in stock imagery provided by Thinkstock are models, and such images are being used for illustrative purposes only. Certain stock imagery © Thinkstock.

ISBN: 978-1-4525-3658-3 (sc)
ISBN: 978-1-4525-3659-0 (e)

Printed in the United States of America

Balboa Press rev. date: 08/03/2011

Dedication

Thanks to my family and friends for helping me produce this book and to the spiritual world for working in the Oneness with me, so that I could share this information with others.

--Wendy Edwards

Acknowledgements

To Ray and my sons for their love, patience and support over the years.

Special thanks to Ray, Joy, Evie and Carolyn for their editing contributions.

To Susanne for her love, guidance and timely generosity.

Special mention to Paula and Mavreen for their spiritual messages of hope and their loving support.

Thanks also to Julie, Joy, Angela, Rachela, Kirsty, Mel, Malgosia, Virginia, Veronica and Laila for their help, encouragement and friendship during the writing of these books.

We are here to love, for all is of love.

Contents

CONTENTS	XI
INTRODUCTION	
My soul's journey	XV
OUR SOUL LIFE	
The human and the soul	3
Understanding the spiritual crisis	7
Soul essence	9
Soul eyes	12
Soul ears	13
Soul nose	15
Soul music	16
Soul colors	18
Soul food	19
Soul unity	21
Souls crossing other dimensions	21
Giving our soul away	23
The soul plates	24
Permanent soul plates	26
Choosing who is on our plate	28
Soul plate size	29
OUR SOUL PATHS	
The Garden of Remembrance	33
The sacred contract	36
The paths	39
Path one	40
Paths two and three	43
Path four	44
Rest and recreation life	47

Lost in the paths	48
Meeting others on the path	49
Lighting the paths	51
Trouble lighting other's paths	53
Blocks to the paths	54
Lessons on the paths	55

KARMIC HEALING

Karma	61
Karma and fate	62
Past-life karma	63
Sacred karmic debt	64
Burning karmic debt	65
Karma across the dimensions	67
Opportunities to balance karma	69
Karma lessons repeating	70
Karmic care of others	72
Karmic poverty	73
Karma affecting having children	75
Karmic stagnation	75
Fragmented karma	76
Quickening karma	77

UNDERSTANDING OUR PAST LIVES

Past lives	81
Past-life illness	82
Fears and phobias from past lives	83
Activating gifts and knowledge from past lives	85
The gifts	86
Future lives	88

CONNECTING TO GUIDANCE

Your guides	93
Respecting your guardians	95
The gatekeeper	96
Time as signs of connection	99

Sensing spirits in the house	101
Asking guides to talk to each other	102
Sharing guides	105
Asking for specific teaching guides	107
Learning in spiritual healing rooms	109
Going to the healing rooms	109
Visiting the learning libraries	111
Asking for better outcomes for others	111

HEALING THROUGH DREAMS

Dreams as spiritual signs	115
Traveling to other places in dreams	118
Meeting those from the other side	118
Sorting out relationships in dreams	120
Meeting your guides	121

THE CREATIVE POWER OF OUR MINDS

The mind/body orbs	125
The thinking brain and the soul mind	127
Spiritual work with the soul mind	129
The universal mind	130
Minds from other dimensions	132
Akashic records	134
Telepathy	135
Calling in telepathically	139
Higher self	141
Changing old mental patterns	144
Tornado	145
Visualization – making it work energetically	147
Feeling your visualization	149

ACCESSING SPIRITUAL DIMENSIONS

Portals	155
The effect of the new openings	157
Spiritual frontiers	160
Soul dimensions	161

THROUGH TIME AND SPACE

Divine timing	167
Spiritual time gateway	169
Magnetic doorways	171
Using energetic wings	172
Space as energy	174

THE SPIRITUAL ENERGY OF MONEY

Money	181
Money cords	183
Past lives and poverty	185
Money discs in aura	186
What if you can't find any discs in your aura	188

IN CONCLUSION

Introduction

My soul's journey

When I turned forty two, I knew something monumental would happen. I had felt that this unspoken fear had been lodged in the recesses of my soul forever. When I had let myself think about it, I had imagined an illness, perhaps a terminal one.

In a strange twist of fate what unfolded was nothing like I had imagined. It was more like the death of who I thought I was, and a renewal of the truth of who I really am, and who I could be. When the life-changing event happened, in some strange way, I was relieved. At last I knew what had been gnawing at me for all those years.

It unfolded on a sunny day. The hum of Saturday filled our house, with the children playing in their bedrooms and the sounds of cars emanating from the road. No-one knew that the defining moment for our family was about to occur. I was busy working on my sewing machine when it happened. Whilst threading the needle with my left hand, and being unaware that the plastic protection on the pedal had broken off, I touched the exposed metal with my right hand. I became electrically attached to the machine, the electric current searing through my body. It surged from one hand to the other, coursing across my heart. It was the longest moment of my life.

All I heard was this incredible scream coming from deep inside my being. This terrible cry of pain, fear and desperation was coming from a place other than me. It was an eerie experience. With no sense of time, I felt myself being thrown backwards, hitting the dining room wall and sliding down onto the slate floor. Slumped on the floor, I could see the machine and cords lying near me. As I looked down, I could see the machine needle lodged in my small finger. Fortunately, the needle had broken and released me from the electrical circuit. I knew the area was unsafe electrically so I pulled myself away and lay twitching and shaking on the nearby wooden floor. I remember thinking "Thank God that I am forty two and still alive."

Over the next few weeks, the full extent of the accident became apparent. The electric shock was so severe that I could not function as before. I lost most muscle function and was unable to lift even a glass. My gait was unsteady, and I looked as though I had suffered a stroke. Driving a car was out of the question, and I was confined to bed.

Life would never be the same, and it took years for me to recover. My job as a teacher was compromised, and my health was delicate to say the least. During the following weeks after the accident, I recognized that my soul's journey had just begun. From then on all I had believed in changed.

Even though the first weeks were dark and scary, I knew I had chosen to return to life on earth. Stamped in my mind was the moment I crossed over and saw my deceased mum and the being of shining light. I remember asking to be allowed to return to my sons, so they could grow up with a mother. It was my strongest wish.

A telepathic conversation happened between my mother and me, and then, in a twinkling I was back in my home. In the days ahead I could feel my mother's presence in the house. In my darkest moments, I knew I could have easily slipped back to the other side. For me, it was a frightening time, having been so near to my own death.

As I look back, I am pleased the year of turning forty two turned out better than I had imagined it would. I was alive, an illness had not claimed me, and I was back with my family.

However, this time of happiness was short-lived. Within months of crossing over I began to deal with my own demons and face the enormity of my true life, my past. Sorting through the terrible reality of my abusive childhood was awful. I began to remember what I had been told by my mother on the other side. She was there to begin the painful process of facing the truth.

Coupled with this was the awakening of my spiritual gifts and chosen path. In healing myself, I came to uncover my own healing and psychic abilities. During the years, I have discovered several gifts and their purpose. This journey has taken me from massage, to healing, channeling and now to writing books.

I believe my return to this life was for a couple of reasons. Firstly, I needed to work through my own personal issues, and secondly, I needed to begin to work with the spiritual ones.

My books have been written with the help of the angels. This is the first book of a series. It is followed by "Spiritual Answers for Health and Happiness" and "Spiritual Answers for Working as a Healing Channel." My soul's journey has not been without its moments, but there has been much learning and growth. I give these words to you now and hope in sharing all I have learnt with you, that your life will be enriched too.

Our Soul Life

Listen with your soul ears for you will hear the truth.
See with your soul eyes and all will be revealed.

The human and the soul

We are both human and soul living on earth. Our soul is eternal, and we are in human form to learn our lessons. Many of us have spent numerous lives on earth, while some of us have been here only a few times. Some of the young souls visiting the earth at this time are adjusting to life in this dimension. The atmosphere here is very dense in comparison to other dimensions, and it can be a struggle. These souls have come to bring new energies and wisdom to our world. Young souls struggle with how we do things in this dimension. Often they voice frustration when they can see better ways to do the same thing. Having lived in other dimensions, our world seems slow and the way we do things somewhat stupid. Time and again, young souls will question why they are here and what it is it all about.

At the same time, old souls have returned to assist and help with the earth changes. Old souls are easy to spot, even when they are babes. They have a certain quality about them, a knowing that exudes from them.

I think we intuitively know on a deeper level, whether we have been on earth many times before, or whether this visit is a relatively new experience for us. It does not matter whether you are an old or young soul. Every visit you make helps you gather more knowledge and learning. I think old souls seem more settled in the earth's atmosphere, as it is familiar to them. After centuries of traveling through the world, they accept the way things operate and can flex with all the complexities of earthly life. This acceptance makes it easier for them to cope with the problems that living in this dimension can create.

Our soul is contained in the human form. Some call it our spirit. It sits in our physical body, flowing out into our aura.

The soul is not confined to time and space like our human form. As a human we can't be in more than one place at a time and our physical body can't move into another dimension. Time also dictates where we are. For example, we can't be in the future or the past.

However, our soul is not bound by these considerations. It can move out of our physical space and travel through other dimensions. This is a new concept to some people. The reason the soul can move is because it is an energy that can leave the physical body. The physical body is very dense, like a heavy weight, so it can't move out of the aura. On the other hand, the soul vibrates at a much higher rate. Therefore, it leaves the aura with ease.

We know on some level that this happens. For example, sometimes when you meditate or just before you fall asleep you can't feel your body. It is like you are floating above the body. It's an unreal feeling. It is then that the soul has lifted out of the aura. The same thing happens when people are in car accidents or suffer trauma. Soldiers or victims of abuse can temporarily leave their physical body until the danger is past. The reason the soul slips out is because it does not want to be damaged. Our soul is, in fact, very delicate, and it can be damaged forever. It has to last through the ages, and so we have learned how to protect it in times of need.

After the trauma has passed, the soul slides back into the physical body, unscathed and intact. For the most part, we re-enter properly, although sometimes we come back in and don't get it quite right. This is when people struggle with post-traumatic stress and other problems. It is because the soul is not sitting correctly in the aura. Occasionally, over time, the soul can re-adjust. If not, healing and energy balancing can help the soul body to sit properly once again in the aura.

Once we understand how differently the human and soul operate on earth it is easier to understand our own life. So, we work from two perspectives, soul and human. The soul has been our vehicle through time and space, while the human form will only last for about eighty years. In our daily lives, we function from both structures. At times we live very much in the human condition, and other times we operate mostly from the soul.

It is important to know that many of us choose to work predominately in one or the other way, either living as a soul in the physical body or as a human with little concern for our soul life. Either way is fine, for each of us is on earth to learn various lessons and either vehicle can assist with our learning.

I am clearly a soul first kind of person. I run my life through my soul body, and, in a sense, my human nature has less to say. Soul first people follow their gut feelings. They tap into their soul for the answers and are often interested in the esoteric aspect of life. All my decisions have to feel right, even if my human side does not agree. In essence, I follow my heart.

Human first people think it through logically using the left side of their brain to come to their conclusions, and their gut feelings are not considered so important. They like to live in the more tangible aspects of life and immerse themselves fully into the humanness of life. If they have an important decision to make the head will win over the heart.

It is not important whether you run your life as soul or human. Nevertheless, it is important that you recognize how you do it as this awareness will help you to understand your life's journey.

Once you work out your own stance, it becomes easy to see where your family and friends are coming from. By understanding those around us, we begin to make sense of it all. I had struggled with this aspect of life before the "lights went on." Now I know who is working through the soul body and who is working through the human one, and I can adapt to how I relate to each person. Before, I was trying to relate to everyone not understanding where they were coming from.

This revelation has made life so much easier. When I am with my soul friends we can talk and share in a soul way, and we talk about our feelings and aspirations. In a sense our souls speak to each other. When I am with my human friends, conversation relates to earthly topics like the family and current events. We can talk about the latest movie or renovating the house, essentially we keep it all very 3D, as I like to call it.

Once I could see who was who, and where I stood in the whole thing, life became less confusing. I could just switch when necessary. I did not change myself all the time, but adjusted myself to the particular situation.

Life on earth can be challenging, yet once I realized this truth it all became simpler. In addition, we all have an inherent order that we are more comfortable with. For example, I am calm and happy to run my life through the soul part. If I always had to use only my human part, I would begin to feel unbalanced. My best balance is soul, then human. Another person might function best expressing their life from a human perspective, rather than soul.

One is no better than the other. It is apples or oranges. It's all to do with the individual. Do it the best way for you, and let others make their own choices.

In different phases of our life, we will also change the order. Sometimes we need to experience the world in very human terms, while another situation might need a soul first approach.

If you decide to be soul first it is important to give balance to your world by incorporating humanness. This could include doing everyday activities and embracing all the human world has to offer. I love to shop for clothes and play around with the material aspects of life, and these things are no less important than meditating.

The importance is the balance we can create - mind, body and soul, each supporting the other.

Finding out where you fit in will bring clarity to your personal life. It will also bring understanding to your other relationships. Knowing who the oranges are, and who are the apples will be enlightening. One of the greatest gifts in life is when you truly understand yourself and those around you.

Understanding the spiritual crisis

A spiritual crisis can occur when there is dysfunction between the human side and the soul. It commonly takes the form of some kind of breakdown and mainly manifests around the time a big decision is about to be made. Our souls decide their purpose in this human life before they come into the earth plane. Some special ones have come to do some extraordinary work. However, once hitting the earth dimension they can forget why they are here and what they agreed to do while on earth. Sometimes, there comes a time when we are supposed to be fulfilling our soul's destiny, except that our human has forgotten. It is then the spiritual crisis can arise.

Spiritual crisis refers to a situation in which we are resisting our true learning or purpose. If we are supposed to be working from a soul perspective and keep living only in the human world, a crisis will emerge. Once on earth we all have free will. Still, souls can become confused and distracted and all manner of things can go wrong when we forget our true purpose.

Functioning from a soul level can make our life more difficult. It is hard to be different, and it is understandable to want to be like everyone else, especially when young. We all want to belong. Added to this, operating through our human side has many benefits. Most importantly, we don't stick out like a sore thumb. By dumbing down our spiritual side, we may make it into the "cool" group. For those of us who have craved acceptance from our childhood, this outcome can be very attractive. Being like everyone else brings with it some comfort and sense of belonging, which is a basic human trait. The human life can also offer some tangible and material gains. In our pursuit of the material, we can receive acceptance and respect from others. Being able to channel or meditate does not hold much power in this space, whereas new cars, holidays and status give us entry to those exclusively human groups.

Having come in with a soul first personality means we have probably inherited our parents' or grandparents' psychic gifts as these gifts generally pass down the line. You may have some issues with these gifts. Maybe you don't want to be psychic or "see" pictures in your head. Just because we are born with the gift does not mean we want it.

On a relationship level, you may be in a loving partnership in which the soul side of you doesn't easily fit. Your partner might think all this spiritual stuff is nonsense. So where does that leave you?

We always have a choice, whether or not we fulfill our purpose on earth. The spiritual crisis comes when we literally have to make that choice, and a battle between the human and soul can take place. In my experience, we generally give ourselves a few chances to follow our soul path before the crisis occurs. The spiritual crisis is our way of waking ourselves up. We would have set it up before we arrived on earth, and if we reached a certain point in time and had not begun our journey, we would have set up an opportunity to do so. Our soul path or life mission was decided in the Garden of Remembrance prior to arriving on earth. I shall speak more about the garden in a later chapter.

Going through a spiritual crisis can be a traumatic time involving emotional turmoil and much angst, as there can be confusion and a sense of being lost. Essentially, we are only coming back to our true selves and returning to our essence. When one resists being a soul person and tries living like a human first, one can create a lot of stress in their life. If you are going through a spiritual crisis the only way out is to recognize what is happening and seek to find your direction and follow your true destiny. During this time remember you have set up this situation to guide you back to yourself.

Soul essence

I believe we all have our individual soul essence. By essence, I mean the inner core of our aura. There are people vibrating at various frequencies and in that way they are dissimilar; but by soul essence, I refer to being made of a different core.

I first encountered this when I had scanned my friend's husband and could psychically see his inner core. I could see an enormous, clear crystal sitting within his aura. It was amazing to see this beautiful, long diamond crystal shining in the middle of his energy body. It was then I realized I was seeing his soul essence. I remembered he had a fascination with crystals and the mineral world. He was even working in the mining industry at the time. Those carrying the crystal essences are seekers of knowledge, especially in the fields of science and technology. Accustomed to past lives where the use of crystals abounded, they are intrigued by all new and revolutionary gadgets. These are typically the inventors of our world. Crystal essences thrive on computer games and all things scientific and are found working in these areas. As crystal essences lived previously in Atlantis and Egypt, they bring with them the gifts and inventions of those advanced civilizations.

Another essence I have witnessed is the angelic essence. Angel essence has a gentle quality to it. There is strength, and it resonates with a thin, fine light. Angel essence is sensitive and soft. Their aural core is like a twinkling, shimmering light. Light emanates from everywhere. It streams out from their core shining into the world. If you could see them psychically they simply shine with a light that seems to have no beginning and no end. At this time, there are many "earth angels" here. They have come to enlighten and help with spiritual growth. Some know their purpose. Some have no idea. Recently, a clairvoyant I know could see the wings emanating from a person on the bus. She was seeing his soul essence. Although he appeared as a young man in an army uniform, he was, in fact, an earth angel. I think he was unaware of his special purpose.

The earth people are here too. The earth essence people are very connected to the earth, and they have a stable, practical quality to them. In past lives, they may have been farmers, nomads or medicine men. Environmental issues and animal rights mainly feature in their life's work. Resilient and down to earth, they are involved with Mother Nature. Usually these souls don't seek the spiritual path like others as they are content just to know the truths of life and live in a simple way. They might champion causes, but not be too worried about personal and spiritual learning.

There are other essences residing on earth at this time whose purpose is unlike the essences above. They originate from Atlantis and Lemuria. These souls are more active politically, and they are to be found organizing change around the globe. At times, it means upheaval and chaos. All around the world we can witness these hot spots. I have noticed that their aura is frequently red with anger and frustration.

Soul essence varies from person to person. When you think of your family and friends you will see the variations. Often we attract our matching essence to us in life, as well as the counterpart. An angelic essence is frequently living with an earth essence. They give strength and balance to each other. Our children may display several essences in the same family group. I believe I have a crystal and an earth in my family.

If you concentrate, you will be able to work out which group you come from.

In the twenty first century, we have an increase in these gifted souls. The world is about to make giant shifts and these souls are in this dimension to help. There are more souls on earth than ever before and each in its way is affecting the earth's vibration.

Soul eyes

We have two levels of seeing, the human eyes and the soul eyes. We all know that we see with our human eyes. We look and our brain tells us what we see. It is a simple mechanism to help us function in the human world. We all use it daily, and it serves us well when we need to work, shop and do emotionless activities.

Soul eyes are different. They refer to a way of looking at the world. When we see with our soul eyes we see what the soul sees, not only what the human sees. I liken it to viewing the world through our spiritual body. Once you begin to activate your soul eyes your ability to see will astound you.

The human sight is from the narrow, human perspective, while soul eyes see all that is. Of course, the soul eyes use the two physical eyes too. We look at someone and we see both from a human and soul level. With soul sight, we have a feeling about what we are seeing, and we sense what is not being shown. Even when presented with a narrow view, we will see it all clearly and have a panoramic understanding of what is really happening. Soul eyes give us the whole picture, and sadly, we might find that all that glistens is not gold.

Looking with soul eyes shines light on what is hidden. These days I am quiet about what I really see. Most of the time it is unnecessary to say a word. If you are with others who only employ human eyes, they won't be able to see what you do, so discussion will be useless. Soul eyes are excellent for doing readings and any energy work and the more you work in this sphere, the greater your sight becomes.

Remember, that when we meet a new person the soul eye contact is very important. On the initial meeting, you read with the soul, as the human has little information to go on.

Everyone has met someone and immediately liked or disliked them due to the soul eye connection. Our eyes truly are the windows to our soul.

Power can be displayed via the soul eyes. Typically, these individuals will almost stare you down in an effort to make you look away. When this used to happen to me, I did not quite understand the dynamics. Now I see the power game being played on a soul level, and it is an interesting revelation to know what the other person is trying to do. Once you work it out you can learn to read much about the supposedly "hidden" soul.

Soul ears

Soul ears work in a similar way to soul eyes, allowing us to hear on a human and soul level. Of course, we can hear the words people say. However, we can also hear what is not being said. Our soul ears help us to hear the subtext, the underlying truth. So when someone says a particular thing, you will hear with human and soul ears. Sometimes both will be delivering the same message, other times you will hear the human one and a different soul one. When we hear in this way, there can be no lies, as we will "hear" it all.

Children come in with highly sensitive soul ears, and they can discriminate between the two messages. Regrettably, over time the gift is lost. Parents and society tell children it is unacceptable to hear the subtext, let alone say it out loud. Many children have been shut down and sent conflicting messages, so by the time they reach puberty most are not listening with their soul ears as it simply gets them confused and into trouble.

We have all listened with our soul ears. An example of this is when your friend may be telling you that they are fine, but you know they aren't fine. You can hear the words they aren't saying. I remember arriving at work and the secretary asking me how I was that day. I answered that I was fine, even though I wasn't. Immediately, she asked me what was wrong.

Our soul ears are one of our greatest assets. Hearing what isn't said gives us clarity and an opportunity to read the situation properly. Learn to listen in this way and try consciously to hear on both levels. Then you will hear the truth.

I believe the reason we have trouble with our ears is due to an energetic blockage. Ear problems relate to blocking out what we don't want to hear or blocking out another person. I am sure this situation can be improved by opening up to others and consciously not blocking.

Our ears are one of the last senses to go before we die, so they are very important in this world. I think both in a human and soul context that they are worth working on.

Psychically, we can easily develop our soul ears. Everyone has ears for hearing, but soul ears can enhance our spiritual connection. Spiritual hearing can be improved by expanding our physical ears. We can begin to visualize seeing our ear chakras become bigger and bigger. When I did it, I saw myself with huge "Mickey Mouse" ears able to catch any sound sent to me spiritually. Over time as you open your "Mickey Mouse" ears more energy can flow in and out and with the increase of energy, your spiritual connection becomes stronger. As our ear chakras open, so will our spiritual abilities advance. Over time, we may find our contact with Spirit grows quickly. Some spiritual workers can literally hear the guide's voice, while others can relay messages because they "hear" them in their mind.

There are people whose soul ears are so well trained they hear the music from other dimensions. How wonderful is that? I had a taste of hearing this music recently. While I was in the shower, I began to hear an entire tune being played in my head. It was amazing. The sound was so clear that I could hear all the instruments in the orchestra. I knew it was Spirit communicating using my new improved soul ears.

Keep opening your soul ears and look forward to the gifts that will come.

Soul nose

Smell is one of the most primitive senses we have. Apparently, it is so strong we record memories onto the sense of smell; so that when we smell a familiar aroma the memories from that time can come flooding back. How incredible! In spiritual work having a good soul nose helps us know when a presence is around. Departed ones regularly use this sense to signal their arrival. You can smell their perfume or their familiar scent and, with just a whiff, you know they are with you. Usually when it first occurs it is a transient experience until you realize what is happening. Not realizing that you are using psychic smell, you may find yourself looking around for a physical reason for the new smell.

I remember when my husband could smell our departed golden retriever in his car. Moses had never been in this vehicle, yet as Ray drove down the road, he began to smell him in the car. At first he wasn't quite sure whether he was just imagining it until he remembered what he had asked for days before. Still upset from his passing, Ray had asked for Moses to send him a sign from the other side, and here it was.

When I wanted to expand my soul nose, I didn't try to make my nose bigger. Rather I worked on the breath. I tried to increase my sensitivity by focusing on the air coming in and out. As the air came in I tried to pick up any smell my soul could recognize. By using this approach you should begin to smell more often, so to speak. Over time, you may begin to smell smoke or particular odors, even though these smells are not in the physical world. In general, they can be signals from Spirit of their presence, or they may come from past lives. When I do readings, I can pick up the smells easily, and I am able to relay this information. Occasionally, the client will also be able to smell the particular spiritual odor being sent.

Soul music

Music is vibration and because we are also vibrating, music has the capacity to move our soul. That is its power. Music is such an important part of our life. Without it, I think we would be lost. Although music is not by nature alive, it is energetically alive. We define a life force as a living thing and so, in a sense, music is alive because it vibrates. To me, it's like the air is moving and carrying the sounds.

Music can transcend time and space. You know when you can hear the song playing over and over in your head. Even though you can hear it, you are aware it is not playing in the real world. Well, a similar phenomenon can happen spiritually when we hear soul music. I have heard whole songs playing in my head. These songs were messages for others, yet they were playing in my head quite clearly. Once I had to sing the song

Spiritual Answers to Guide Your Life

out loud so my friend could tell me what it was called. Soul music can reach us in bizarre ways.

Hearing a particular piece can take us back to a special time or significant memory. In my experience, the spiritual world will regularly use music to send me a sign. Mostly, it works like this. I may have asked for help and then, for the first time, a song plays and I really hear the words. The song will give me all the answers to my question. It's an amazing way to communicate. Quite frequently people from the other side can also "talk" to us through music. My deceased mum always plays a particular song, her song, then I know she is saying hello.

Soul music has another quality. It can heal. During difficult times, we will be drawn to certain music and gain comfort from listening to it. In these cases, the music heals our soul. Normally, we will want to hear it repeatedly until that part of us is healed. Before I dealt with my issues, I never recognized the importance some music had in helping me release those deeper emotions. These days when I listen to the words, I hear what my soul voice was trying to say. If you go back and listen to your "soul" music you will gain insights to those times.

Soul music can move our aura energetically. When we listen to heavy rock music the base and sacral chakras are activated. That is why young sexually developing adults are drawn to this music, as it makes the lower chakras come alive. This music can help to lift the energy of the aura and make us vibrate more strongly.

Romantic music affects the emotions, especially the heart and the throat chakras. It helps with the flow of energy around the body, soothing the emotions and calming the soul. Romantic songs allow our loving feelings to be expressed and encourage a deeper level of universal love to resonate in us.

Classical music is good for increasing our vibration. It is useful when we are engaged in meditation and spiritual work. Many people suggest you use it when you are studying as it helps you to access the information. This is because classical music activates the third eye and crown chakra, which are directly connected with the mind.

If you are feeling down, play plenty of rock music and feel the difference. Conversely, if you need to feel calmer use classical and romantic music. Soul music is an important part of life, so remember to use it to enhance and give your energy body what it needs.

Soul colors

Soul colors refer to the colors we are drawn to in life. Our aura is made up of a multitude of colors. I believe some colors present in our aura are from this world and there are some colors we can't yet see in our earthly world. When we see a color on earth it comes through into our human eyes. Our pineal gland literally takes in colors. This gland can manipulate light and use it to feed our aura so that it can enter the body energetically. In seeing the colors, we also absorb them energetically. In a sense the colors feed our soul.

People are color conscious and I think we are drawn to specific colors for various reasons. On a level, we know the colors that our aura needs. The clothes we wear have a color vibration, and this vibration directly alters our aura. For example, your aura may need more green or blue to remain healthy, or maybe you need to alter your vibration by adding more of one color. I think those who choose lots of black have many dark areas already in their aura. This does not mean they are bad. It can signify negative thought forms or dark times recorded in their energy field.

If our base chakra requires more red to run well, we might find we choose to wear lots of red-colored clothes or surround ourselves in a red environment. This may happen until we have accessed enough of the particular color required.

Everyone knows the best colors for them. So choose from your heart when you color your world.

As you ascend spiritually, your choice of colors will alter. Old clothes or home décor might not resonate well any more. Be aware of this and change accordingly. If the blue room bugs you, and you crave yellow, take it as a sign of moving forward. It is human nature to hang on to things, and we can all resist change. Just remember that the colors around us directly influence us on a soul level.

Soul food

Food is sustenance and we need it to function on earth. Some people believe we don't necessarily need food, and that we should be able to survive by accessing energy instead. Although I am sure this could be true, especially in the future when we will all be more advanced, I must admit I am still quite enjoying the food experience. For me and many others, eating is more than surviving, as food fills many other needs.

Soul eating is different from the human physical eating because it feeds our soul. Soul foods always have some emotional attachments. For example, the stew our mum used to make or the cakes we loved as a child.

Some soul food can come from past lives. You may have a love of Thai or Mexican cuisine, and this love may come from a previous life in that country. People are drawn to foods they have enjoyed in other lives. In general, foods they dislike can originate from these past connections. Maybe you spent a lifetime only eating potatoes and very little else, so this experience could have put you off potatoes forever.

Soul food feels familiar and comforting. People may think soul food means sweets and take away, but I think it is not the same for each person. The reason soul food is relevant is the effect it has on our digestion. Soul food goes down easily. Its energy feeds our energy body, and, even if those chips or chocolate are nutritionally poor, they will support the soul. Soul foods soothe us like other foods don't. That is why people tuck into ice-cream and salty nuts when they are searching for comfort. Carrots and eggs may just not do it. I don't advocate eating lots of junk food. Nevertheless, sometimes no other food will do. Stop punishing yourself and see that by eating these foods you are truly soothing your soul.

Soul food can be signs for us. Food can alert us to what is happening on a deeper level. When you see yourself reaching for some foods be observant. If you are eating loads of "kiddie" food, maybe your little child needs more healing. If you are trawling through stormy waters when dealing with your childhood, let yourself eat like a child. Buy yourself an ice-cream in a cone and know you are feeding the child within.

Soul food has many layers. Some are good, while others are signs for us if we choose to look. I noticed I ate soul foods when I was trying to suppress anger. It was a total revelation to me. As a child I was not allowed to express anger, and I had used food to hold my feelings down. In the past, it was a necessary crutch, but now I can be angry and express it.

Once we embark on the soul food trail much learning can occur. Some foods are purely comforting, while with other foods, its role is to suppress deeper emotions. Our soul talks to us each day. Learning to hear our inner voice will bring many understandings, and if we look behind our choices, maybe we may uncover the truth. Anger, fear and loss consistently underpin soul eating. I found that once I recognized my patterns my soul could begin to heal.

Soul unity

We may like to think we only affect our own little world, but this is untrue for all of our actions have a direct vibrational effect on others. What happens in our backyard resonates throughout the universe. This is a positive and negative aspect of universal law.

The negative aspect is obvious, because the fear, hate and anger in other people can permeate our auras and lower our own vibrations. Still, on the brighter side the positive part is that as we raise our own vibration, so the world's vibration is also raised. The earth's vibration has been directly increased by all the work done by individuals raising their own vibration. In the past, the monks and gurus knew about energy. They prayed and meditated in order to raise the vibrations and in their own quiet way they were already preparing the world for change.

Keep working on your own development because you are helping the world in raising its vibration. With higher vibration, you become closer to the celestial beings and the knowledge stored above.

Souls crossing other dimensions

Only on earth are we bound by time and space. We are actually able to move anywhere and at any time on a soul level. Even so, as humans this can be a hard concept to grasp.

When I do a reading and someone's relative who has crossed over talks to me, I am working in the soul dimension. I am not tapping into my human side to connect. My human side is unable to do the connection. Only the soul can.

Just like the person who has crossed over can travel, so can we. It is only our rational mind stopping us as we let ourselves be bound by time and space. However, once we release ourselves from that concept everything is possible.

I believe there is no time. It all happens at the same "time." It looks like a layered cake, like one lifetime upon another, each impacting on the other. These lives are all happening in the same universal time and space. Once you grasp this idea of the layers one on top of the other, like a cake, it becomes very exciting. As all the lives are happening at the same time any work we do on one life will directly influence all the others.

For example, say you are working on releasing anger from your aura in this life. Well, in reality, you would be affecting your other lives. Of course, to strengthen the outcomes we could focus on all our lives when we do release work, and it will filter into all the layers. We can simply work on something now and clear it out in the past and for the future. Wow, I got really fascinated by that concept!

You may wonder why you would even bother because there are so many other things to do here on earth. The reason it is important to do this kind of clearing is the impact it makes on your potential other lives. By sorting out your issues and karma now, may stop you from dragging it all with you into the next life. You can finally complete the lesson. I chose not to have any more lives with my father, so instead of leaving the lessons for when I passed, I have chosen to deal with them here.

Although it is harder to work in earth's denser vibration the rewards are greater. By doing the work on earth, it frees you up to focus on other lessons when you cross over. Generally, when you cross over much time is spent in the healing rooms where you look at your life and debrief. By working in this dimension on many issues you can fast-track and don't need to spend so long in the healing rooms. This means you can advance your own progress and begin your work on the other side sooner.

I admit that doing the work is very challenging as the energy is much denser and the rewards unclear. Still, with faith and good intentions much work can be done before we die and move into the next dimension. Our soul has greater capacities than we can ever imagine. All we need is faith and guidance, for all is possible in the eyes of Spirit.

Giving our soul away

The idea of being able to sell our soul or give it away has been a cultural belief, and throughout the ages, it has been touted as a possibility. All we really have is our soul, as our soul is all of us and without it, we don't exist. Therefore, the concept of selling or giving it away is an interesting one.

In energetic terms our soul is a pure, vibrating energy. In my opinion, I believe no one can take our soul away. They can only take or own some of our energy field. The idea of giving our soul away refers to us giving away some of our energy to another, like a power exchange in which one submits or gives to the other. I think it is more to do with a power issue, not complete soul ownership. We have all seen others submit and relinquish their power or energy to others. It happens every day. People are always giving their energy and power to others.

There can be a power imbalance between souls. Sometimes, due to karma, there is a debt to be paid. However, this is not the same as giving our energy away.

There can never be ownership of one's soul because our soul is part of God, we are part of God. It just is, and through time and space, it remains itself. No one can ever own your soul. The idea of owning something or someone is a human construct, a human constraint. Just remember, in the world of universal Spirit the soul can only belong to the wholeness of the Light, and all there is.

The soul plates

Relationships can be very complex at the best of times. We all spend most of our life consumed with the way our relationships are affecting our lives. Our relationships run on two levels simultaneously, one being the human aspect and the other being the soul relationship we have with a person. Even though people may think the relationship is on the human level, much more is clearly happening in the soul department. Most of our relationships have a very powerful soul base. Too often we view our relationships in a limited way, not acknowledging the power of the soul aspect.

Over time, I have been psychically shown a visual of how our relationships operate on a soul level. It is so interesting and very different to what I had been led to believe. Apparently, we all exist on what I will call soul plates. These are energetic plates underpinning our lives.

I found the idea easy to comprehend and could easily imagine myself standing on my own plate. I could also see others standing each on their own plate. Then, when we meet someone, I could see both plates overlap, and therefore, we would directly influence each other. When I began to view the soul plates in this manner, I could understand that what was happening on one plate would affect the other plate, and vice versa.

In our human world, we have been taught to understand relationships in a very different way. On earth, we are supposed to obey certain rules, and many people have boundaries around them. Human friendships and families are supposed to follow predestined paths.

However, I discovered the soul plates follow different spiritual laws to the human ones. For a start, there is much flexibility with soul plates as you don't have to conform to social conventions. The usual regulations and controls are put aside. Using soul plates is liberating as you can move your soul plates and slide out of each other's space without any repercussions. Unlike human relationships, you are free to explore other relationships and pursuits without being punished. For example, if someone chooses to veer off and out of your sphere forever, it is understood and accepted.

The plates are designed to move to assist in our spiritual growth. Unfettered by human constraints, much soul growth can be made. I believe if we all understood the soul plates as the fundamental basis of relationships, life would flow more easily. The constant movement in our social world would also make more sense, and instead of seeing change as a threat or mistake, we would see it as liberating for all.

I loved the concept of the soul plates sliding back and forth. Even though it seemed like a new idea to me, it was already happening in most of our lives. We have all definitely used the soul plates in various relationships. We just haven't fully realized what we have been doing. You will know the relationships I mean. For example, you would have people who you may not have seen for ages then when you meet you both pick up where you left off. The two soul plates slide onto each other, connect for a short time, and move off. These are genuine soul connections.

I have thought a great deal about working in relationships using these soul plates. If we could all work on this level everyone would have much more freedom in their lives. There would be an end to others trying to control, guilt trip or coerce another. Added to that, we could let others go in the knowledge they may need to leave for a while and be happy about it.

With this information, I started to examine my way of relating to others and letting the soul relationship take over the human one. I had to work hard at letting go of my old habits. Living my life in this new way was not always easy, but it all made sense to me, and it felt like a truly loving way to embrace my family and friends.

You may still have the emotions associated with the plates moving away; just remember it is all part of your spiritual growth. Once we can begin to live our life in this way the soul can ascend. Never forget that God gives us free will, so we need to give it to others and ourselves. It is a gift of unconditional love.

Permanent soul plates

Permanent soul plates refer to plates that can glide in and out, yet are constantly attached to each other by an energetic cord. Normally, these plates and cord connections exist with people who are in our intimate grouping, like family and close friends. In these cases when they float off and away, there remains an energetic link between both plates, the cord hanging on energetically. Hardly anyone ever speaks about it; however, we all feel the connection is still there even when our plates are far apart. What we are sensing is the energy exchange between the two plates. Although we might be separated by time and space, we feel the other person, as if they were still overlapping our daily lives.

In general life, disagreements may occur, and people can stop communicating in the human world, but the plates continue to talk energetically. You know the friends who are angry with you and haven't rung back. Even though their plate may have spun off away from you, they are very much in your daily life, especially energetically. You can feel them in your mind, and in your heart.

I have realized these permanent discs remain well after the person's last breath. This is because energy never dies, so in death the connection remains. There are times in life when things happen that can't be resolved in the human world. In the soul world, the door remains ajar waiting for the right time. I never give up on these souls, especially if I have great love for them. You can never know when the soul plates will eventually overlap again. There may be an opportunity this lifetime, once they cross to the other side, or we may have to wait for a few lifetimes. Sooner or later, we all know the time will come, and if it is meant to be, the plates will move across, and we can be together again to sort out what needs to be sorted.

I try to understand and live with the reality of soul plates in my life. I know who the permanent ones are, and if you look around in your life you will know them too. Try to allow others to follow their own course, and if it means you can't be together, let them go in love. For isn't unconditional love the greatest love of all?

Choosing who is on our plate

As in all things in life, we have free will. It is important that we choose who shares our soul plates. In a sense it is still our space, and so we have the power to decide who is in our world. It is wise to remember that just because someone is on our plate it does not give them permission to run our life. Conversely, being on someone else's plate does not give us the right to try and control their lives.

The plates may connect, but you always have free will. I have heard people lament that they have no choice, as they have to do it the family's way. In reality, we always have choices. I did find when I began to make boundaries with controlling family members and friends, I was not popular. It might mean that when we exercise free will, they dislike us for a time. Then again, by making these choices, we are liberating others to do the same.

With this knowledge, you can choose who is in your world and who isn't. If you need to let some plates go for a time, be assured the world won't come to a grinding halt. You can even disconnect from everyone and whirl around on your own plate until you want to come back.

When you try another approach it can be difficult and those around you may resist. In spite of this, our actions often empower others by teaching them how to fend for themselves and draw upon their own resources. As well, in setting boundaries, we teach others to do, likewise.

In the end, we all know whom we want to be with. We also know whom we might have to be with. In deciding soul plate access, this knowledge will influence our choices.

In life, the plates constantly move around. Mostly, I sense whose plate is moving in or out. Sometimes it is their decision, sometimes mine. Just because they come into our field, it does not mean that you have no say. There are some people who will always be on your soul plate. It is the choice you have made already. It may be your children, your parents or a true friend. We all have individuals in our lives who are permanently there.

However, others may have swung in uninvited, so to speak. In these situations, we can choose. Whether they sit on our plate becomes a two-way decision. Remember, this is our space, our soul plate, and as such we can decide who sits with us.

Soul plate size

Working out our personal soul plate size is a valuable lesson because they are not all the same. Some individuals have huge plates capable of carrying layers of other plates. You know the people I mean. They are the ones with an enormous number of people in their lives. When I see them, I wonder how they manage it, yet somehow they do. Others, probably like me, can only handle so much before feeling overloaded. If you think about it, you will instinctively know where you stand.

I don't think either one is good or bad. It just is.

If you are one of those people with countless companions society would refer to you as being a "people person." If you have less, sometimes, you are labeled a "loner." Once I worked out where I was in the scheme of things I could understand myself better.

For true contentment and peace, you should try to aim to have the optimum soul plates for you. Until I came upon this information, I was unaware of my own needs. Only with this understanding did it all make sense to me. I realized I could actively work at having the right number of people on my own soul plate. By tapping into this knowledge, I could monitor my life. If I was overwhelmed, I could lessen my world. If I felt I was missing out, it was time to gather more plates.

We all take stock at times and review our relationships. Maybe you could ask yourself whether you need to lessen your plate load and retreat for a while, or add to your plate. Once you look at your world in this way you can get the balance you need.

In addition, you may want to recognize your changing needs. I noticed that in some parts of my life, I wanted to have more people around than other parts. When you are very busy with work or are beginning a new romantic relationship your plate can be quite barren in terms of other relationships. Going through an illness or grief can affect you too. Acknowledging these different stages on our path will help us keep track of where we want to be.

Our Soul Paths

Walk your own path,
while holding the hands of those you love.

The Garden of Remembrance

The Garden of Remembrance exists in the ethereal planes, and it is there that we decided our life's mission. Before we arrived on earth we sat with other light beings and planned our visions for this next life. However, once we entered the earth plane the memories of this time were erased and most of us have no memory of our visit, let alone the plans we made.

It is important to realize that we planned our life because it means that what happens to us is what we wanted to happen. In the garden, we set out several paths and many choices for our present life. When I first realized I had agreed to the life I had lived, it was a bitter pill to swallow. I mean parts of my life had been awful, and it took time for me to come to terms with my new reality, and the fact I had really agreed to all that had occurred in my life. Therefore, I suggest you take time to come to this understanding of your life's paths.

People unfairly blame other people, God or the universe, for their difficult times. Just the same, on a universal level it does not work that way. We planned our lessons and paths; we cannot blame anyone else. I think to take responsibility for that can be quite challenging, especially for our human side.

In the garden, we decided who we would meet, where it would be and when it would occur. Of course, we did leave some room for us to move and negotiate. Still, we set it all up. When we made the plans in the garden, we made it through our soul mind. We were not constricted by the human mind or the denseness of earth.

Now the soul can be like a big bulldozer, as it knows what has to be achieved and the lessons to be learned. I am sure my guardians tried to explain how hard various things I had chosen to do were going to be. However, I think I was not thinking about the human condition there in the garden. I am sure my soul just took over and thought it would all be fine.

Once on earth most of us realize that we have bitten off more than we can chew and feel that back in the garden we may have opted for more challenges than we should have. The human always opts for the easiest and least painful journey. It goes with being human and feeds our way of thinking, which is predominately based on fear. Given that, I feel that we are still human and ought to be kind, rather than harsh on ourselves. It has been said that we never ask for more than we can carry, and I do believe this to be true, but that is not how it feels some days. Whilst working through hard times may feel lonely and difficult, please remember that you are never alone. Help is always available to you if you seek it.

When things are tough try to avoid the "victim attitude" because nothing is ever "done" to you. All is as it needs to be. Keep in mind that somewhere back in the garden these lessons were put in place by you and your guides.

I own all of my life. I am not a victim. Only if I refuse to learn the lesson do I become one, a victim of my own making. When I struggle with life I ask myself what am I supposed to learn from this event, what have I set up to look at in my life? Then I can focus on my learning and not get bogged down in feeling sorry for myself. Of course, it is normal to whine and complain, and so I just let it be over quickly, so I can move ahead and do the lesson.

Sometimes, we will set a very difficult life with considerable growth. Other lives can be what I refer to as the rest and recreation life, an easy, non-taxing path. You may have met some people opting for this life. Everything goes smoothly. It is simple with no dramas or big lessons for them. The rest and recreation life is like a pit stop. Maybe you have some friends enjoying the rest and recreation lives. One of my dearest friends has been sailing through and enjoying this kind of life. My life, on the other hand, has been like a never-ending soapie, while her life has been calm and without many dramas.

Initially, I did not get it, and I could not understand why her life was so easy and mine seemed so rocky. Now it all makes sense. I had not chosen the rest and recreation life, she had. Having her with me has been wonderful. Her support and love have made it so much more bearable, maybe more for me than for her. Treasure such friendships. These souls have chosen to spend their lives helping us with ours. They can be the calm in our storm. What a gift, what a love!

There is another life choice I call the compressed one. It seems like the rest and recreation life. All goes well at the beginning of the person's life. Everything is lovely and without problems. Then, at a designated time, all hell breaks loose. Instead of having the difficulties spread out, in this life we opt for a condensed version. Normally, we choose the compressed life when we want to burn lots of karma in a few months or years, instead of spreading it out over a life-time. I believe all the parties involved would have agreed to this compressed version. We would have witnessed families dealing with one thing after the other. In general, with the compressed version, life becomes very challenging and everything seems to happen all at once.

The compressed life is extremely difficult because we have little or no time to recover. When you set this life up you would have placed people around you to give assistance. Remember to recognize who they are. Keep in mind that you don't have to do it all alone. Friends, family and health practitioners of all kinds are always near, so use the support available.

Our spiritual guardians are there waiting for our call. Much help can be given by these wonderful beings. Ask for assistance regularly, and try to connect with them to receive healing and guidance. Remember, support can be given by those in other dimensions, including loved ones who are no longer earth-bound. In my readings, ancestors from people's families have come forward offering help. Quite often these ancestors were unknown to the person I was reading. A couple of times, I could see lines of relatives from the person's extended family waiting to help, so ask, and you will receive.

I have frequently made a joke about the life I have chosen this time, remarking that next life before I come down, I will definitely read the small print. I feel my soul made choices my human has struggled with. You might have times here when you feel like me. Still, through it all, I know I can find my way and so can you.

Think of the Garden of Remembrance with love and reverence. It is a wondrous place. Here is where your journey began and here is where it will end, in a place of light and love.

The sacred contract

Some of us would have made our sacred contract in the Garden of Remembrance. The sacred contract is a promise made when we were in spirit form. If you have made a sacred contract it would be activating in this life. Universally, the contract is similar to a promise. As with many promises, not all are honored.

Some promises are karmic in nature. These promises are to others to balance or repay karma. However, the sacred promise is not like the karmic promise. In my understanding, sacred contracts are specifically made for spiritual endeavors. You would have agreed to fulfill a particular mission, like being a healer or advancing some area using spiritual means. When I speak of it being spiritual work, I mean coming from a spiritual intention. It does not have to be only in a spiritual area like healing or Reiki. Our sacred contract can be work we will do in society like science, finance or beginning a particular project. Part of our sacred contract could be in supporting a project to take off and be successful. A sacred contract made in the Garden of Remembrance holds much weight. It is not to be taken lightly. It is a promise to serve the bearers of the Light while on earth.

Of course, we don't have to do it. I have met lots of people who just couldn't go through with the contract once they arrived here. Often these people needed to sort through their own stuff, face their issues and heal before they could begin their real work. Given the challenge of all that personal work, many simply walked away. Maybe they will honor their promise another time. I do believe our own issues need to be cleared before the real work begins and honestly, that part can be extremely hard.

The sacred vow usually involves contracts made to support others too, and I have found that along the way, desertion is a very real outcome. Perhaps we were supposed to work with someone, and then they decided not to do it with us. In these situations, their decision will directly affect our plans to complete our contract. Once they leave, it takes time and new resources before we can follow the path again.

During the years, I have always felt a strong drive to do the work, while others around me have not shared my enthusiasm. I have met countless readers and healers who have chosen to move back into the mainstream. In retrospect, I think several of them were meant to work with me, and now their decision has changed my course too. We may have to accept other's choices if they don't want to carry out the work. Spirit will send in replacements. It just takes time.

The sacred contract directly affects marriages and long-term partnerships. If it was written that our partner was supposed to work with us on the same project and chooses otherwise, the whole plan goes astray. Unfortunately, I have also discovered that if one person is steaming ahead, while the other one is far behind, the relationship can get out of sync. This poses a real threat both to the relationship and the promise made. The same thing can happen in relationships at work.

We always have free will, even when a sacred contract is agreed on. I believe there is little point in giving up, as we will probably have to come back in another life to do it all again. I would rather soldier through it this time.

We will know if we are one of the sacred contract groups. By understanding the setup, we will be able to understand our strong conviction in the work we have to complete. I believe it was easier once my head understood what my soul already knew, that we are a complimentary team working together for the same goal. Although I understood my vow it took time for my sacred work to unfold, and I had to wait for guidance and assistance along the way. Our spiritual helpers are clever as they choose to show us step by step. I think if they revealed everything from the beginning it might be too much to comprehend, and we might run away.

Enjoy your service work as it unfolds. Eventually, as you look back, you will marvel at how beautifully it has been designed, and you will be pleased you stayed and completed your sacred contract.

The paths

During each life on earth, we have several paths we can choose. Before entering the earth plane, we planned these routes. Nonetheless, once we leave the Garden of Remembrance all can be forgotten. The paths rank from the easiest and least productive life, to the one giving us the greatest spiritual and personal growth. The paths in between are like half-way houses with varying degrees of difficulty. Some people opt for three paths, while others have four. It does not matter how many paths each of us has. The first real challenge is to recognize that these paths exist. The second is to understand what path we are on during various stages of our life.

Our time on earth is all about the lessons we have set for ourselves. In the human form, we can learn many soul lessons and achieve great spiritual growth. The quest is all about personal and spiritual growth. It is not about money, status and power. Once we understand why we have chosen to be here, we can advance more rapidly. We have planned all of our lessons and the various paths we can travel. The people we need to meet are waiting along the way. The gifts we need to embrace will emerge as we grow.

Many earthbound people want to blame others for all the bad things that happen. They have forgotten their time in the Garden of Remembrance. In that place, we set out our lessons and the obstacles that we wished to surmount. We chose the people who would help us learn these lessons, and we set up our paths.

Regardless, most of us have forgotten this time. Once we remember the reasons we chose to come to earth, we will be closer to our God than we could have imagined. Coming home means seeing the way our universe really operates. Our happiness is directly connected to this understanding. No longer do things happen to you. There are no failures, only lessons. Each person with whom we come into contact has a learning to give us.

Some people are with us due to karmic connections, as we have all chosen the connection for mutual learning. Often, once the lesson is learnt, either the person moves on or the relationship moves to another level. Many souls have chosen to burn off a lot of karma at this time. There is a quickening throughout the world, a speed in communication, and this applies not only in the physical world. The internet is symbolic of a rapid change in communication in our daily relationships. On a personal level, many of us are speeding along our paths and learning our lessons quickly.

The paths are a fascinating avenue for growth. They give us personal power to evolve and develop in ways we never dreamt possible.

Path one

The first path seems like the easiest, and in a way it is. However, life cannot progress much on path one, except on a human level. The focus is on worldly issues. How one looks, what one owns and one's position in society overrides everything else. On this path one judges and is judged by others, and there can be much "fakeness" as everyone tries to project the "right" image.

Power and control are major features on this path since these attributes are seen as valuable. No one works on improving themselves on a soul level at all for everything is on a human level. Denial is a common thread in path one, as dealing with one's issues would be too challenging. People

Spiritual Answers to Guide Your Life

essentially hide here because it can seem like a safe place. You can be sure no one else on path one wants to dig deep and face their issues either. Once in this place one is forced to link into the mindset of the group because individuals are not well-tolerated as they are a threat to the status quo.

Mostly, people who suffer with addictions will frequent this plane. Denial fits in well and one can stay in the same place and no-one minds. Addiction is tolerated because through the use of food, cigarettes and drugs outstanding and deep-seated emotions are suppressed to avoid dealing with difficult memories or traumas. People who have grown up in harsh environments will feel comfortable on path one, while others who have lived in punitive homes will welcome the lax ways.

There appears to be little structure except, I have noticed there is an unspoken rule. Basically, one is expected not to rock the boat. When one chooses to live on this path one constantly meets people similar to them. The people have different names, but they are all the same. Everyone vibrates at the same rate, and all carry similar unresolved issues and dark baggage. There is little light and much inner confusion for people on this path. There are no long-term goals, only transient ones that beg to be met. Sadly, with all things transient, satisfaction is small and short-lived. These people dream about a better future except, they make no move to activate it. Much time is spent waiting for someone else to fix it all up. It feels that life is unfair and that a cruel blow has been dealt.

Here not much soul growth occurs. I liken it to being on the merry-go-round, you go around a lot, yet in spite of this you go nowhere.

It is not our role to judge others if they decide to experience this trip. We all make our choices. Some stay on this path because it is easy. For others, it is a starting point. Young souls frequent this plane to gain wisdom and an understanding of how the earth works. These souls can choose to start working on some difficult life lessons, especially if they need the earth experience as a platform for the work they have come down to do. Knowledge can be gained by experimenting in drugs, alcohol or crime. Living this life will bring with it a deeper understanding of the issues that people can encounter, and so these souls can develop the necessary compassion. Experience is the best teacher and on this route, they can gain wisdom. In time these souls move out and onto their next path. It is merely a learning path for them. Often later, these souls will work with others who have been lost on the path. They may become counselors, youth workers; work in shelters or in drug and alcohol rehabilitation.

Sadly, though, the majority of people never progress and can spend lifetimes on path one. Many people on path one fail to accept responsibility for their own lives, and therefore, cease to learn. The people who inhabit this path regularly act like victims. We can find the real victims of abuse hiding on this path. Survivors are not welcome in this place as they present too much of a threat, so anyone wishing to deal with anything will need to move to the next path.

Normally, people existing on path one will be challenged by others from paths two and three. The universe is constantly sending in others to encourage us to ascend. People will come in and try to encourage movement ahead, but if there is no hope of advancement those from path two, three or four will move on. We have all been with others on this path. I have observed that these people really don't want to move. When they are given the chance to move up to path two, many will resort to their old ways and stay.

Path one is a good place to begin when learning about the human world. On the other hand, I don't believe it is the best path for growth.

Paths two and three

The next two levels can blend together and seem like the same, although they are slightly different. On path three there are more opportunities for personal and spiritual growth, than on path two. Some people can move back and forth from one path to the other. It is like there is a bridge between the paths. Some of the lessons may be similar, just with varying degrees of difficulty.

The outcomes in life are dependent on which path we mostly frequent. Normally, there will be the same people on both paths, while at other times one will only encounter them on the separate paths. I think that paths two and three allow much more flexibility than path one and four. People seem to be able to cross back and forth easily as there are open gates along the way. These paths give a variety of opportunities and choices. In some ways that can be good, although whilst tracking back and forth specific issues may not be addressed. That can be one of the challenges of working on these levels.

People working on their highest path will occasionally take refuge in path two or three. In general, this will be in times of great stress or illness and won't be for long. Vibrating at the high level required for path four makes it hard to stay on a lower path. It is a similar experience for those on paths two and three. One may also slip back to path one when tired or ill. This can be a trap for some people, as it will feel comfortable, and they may be unwilling to step up again.

Paths two and three are separated by an easier route. That is why people crisscross more regularly. The leap to the highest path is harder because it is like crossing a chasm, so there is more incentive to remain on path four.

The majority of people live on paths two and three. Here they can live in the more material, superficial life and only sort out things when they feel like it. There is less urgency to work off karma or face lessons.

If level one was sitting still, this is walking. On the highest path, one will need to sprint and jump some hurdles.

Paths two and three are okay, but there is always that yearning. The yearning comes from one's soul, from not being on the highest path. Some lessons will be worked out, and a moderately good life lived, but it will feel at times, as though one is just going through the motions.

Path four

Path four is the highest, the hardest and the most satisfying path, in my opinion. On this path, we feel connected to our soul. It is like the light inside you is finally switched on and on a deep level, you know who you are, and what you need to do. On path four we live the greatest purpose of our life. At times it will feel daunting, yet it is, as if we are truly alive. Now we can fulfill our true destiny. To me, it feels like I have finally come home to myself.

To think this is the easiest path is a mistake, but it is the most rewarding. On this path, the trail is steep and hard. There are countless lessons to learn and constant personal challenges to deal with. In a sense the learning never ends. I believe we can only truly serve our soul's purpose when we work at our highest level. On path four there is the opportunity for enormous growth and rapid change.

On the highest path, I have found my spiritual connection to be extremely important. I feel guided by my inner voice and close to my spiritual guardians. I know I am on track. In my human world, some people are critical of my choices, especially those on other paths. However, I know that if I stand by what I intuitively feel, I can't go wrong.

On this path, you may pursue meditation, yoga and be actively working on personal growth. You will find life very exciting, as you explore new horizons and are constantly learning. There will always be something to work on or ideas to explore. It's a never-ending process.

Socially, you may realize that you are not as popular as before. You may spend more time alone and being in the company of others may not thrill you as much. I noticed I could often feel out of place and would soon bore of the conversation. It was as though my shift had created a shift in my social world, subtle, but nonetheless, powerful. I could no longer spend hours talking about subjects I found less interesting to me. It was a shift that I took a while to be comfortable with.

It is okay to be in one's own company and spend less time in mainstream. Invitations once automatically accepted may now present problems. Remember, if it does not feel right for you, then it isn't. Only attend social functions when you really want to because the time for doing the "right thing" is over. Be polite when you refuse, knowing there is no need to explain why. Once you start to say "no" to these events you will feel a sense of relief. Honestly, I found it truly liberating.

Your social world might shrink for several years when you move up onto the highest path. Time is frequently given for you to spend more time alone, enabling you to work more quickly through your issues. During these times, you may almost feel like you are on some kind of retreat, except instead of being on a hill side in Nepal, you are tucked away in your little house in suburbia. This time ends, so be patient.

Some people have an illness or lose their jobs, so they have to stop. In this way, they are being given time to shift to the higher path. During this process, you can feel lost and unsure. You will, at times, feel like you are in a mess, both mentally and emotionally. Have faith, for all will be made clear, just ride the wave until you come into calm water.

There is generally a money shortage at this time and that adds even more pressure. To follow the higher path regularly entails an initial drop in income and status, and this can be hard to handle as money gives us power and security. Occasionally, this drop in money can be for a long time. It may be necessary for us not to be working in order to move in another direction. Once we let go of the money strings, we will be free to make personal changes. At this time, learning the difference between what we need, and what we want, is enlightening.

The loss of income can mean the loss of status. I think getting money is easier than getting status. Although our society loves money, I think it loves status even more. Status is like an external pat on the back, a bit like a power trip. Unfortunately, if we choose the highest path less people may value our choices, and our status may drop. In a world that measures success in terms of having lots of money and being employed in a powerful job, being able to connect to the spiritual world or dealing with our personal issues holds little weight.

If we choose this path we will generally go alone. We must support ourselves at this time, and not seek approval from others. They will be coming from another place, and their judgment will be based on different things.

Path four can be like being out in the desert on our own. Yet, like the desert, it has a beauty of its own, a freedom. For the sense of peace and personal happiness, I think it is worth it.

Rest and recreation life

Every four or five lives we opt for the rest and recreation life. After dealing with many of our lessons we give ourselves a break. During this life things go pretty easily with no real dramas and no great learning. It's like a "breather" along the way. These paths are set up in a similar way to the other paths, except that they are not as challenging.

As I mentioned in an earlier chapter, we can recognize the people who are on a rest and recreation life because they seem to have very good lives. While we are struggling with constant dramas, they just breeze through life. There seems to be very few difficulties in their world. They have enough love, money and plenty of opportunities.

It can feel weird when our own life is so contrasting, but don't despair, for in time we will reach the rest and recreation life too. As a rule, we have a support person with us who is experiencing the rest and recreation life, while we are living in the soap opera one. It is good to have these souls to travel along the journey with us, as they create stability. The paths in this life are fairly similar. Few challenges will arise on them, and it is only a matter of personal choice which one we opt for.

Rest and recreation lives are a chance to recuperate and enjoy the human experience. It's like sitting in the middle of the see-saw instead of the two ends, so there are few ups and downs. Family life is normal and without too many dramas and there is enough work, money and usually plenty of travel to enjoy. Time is made available for creative pursuits and fun activities. All in all, it's a great human and spiritual holiday.

When I first encountered people living these lives, I could not understand it. Why was my life full of challenges and theirs so easy? Was there a lesson for me?

Now that I know the way the paths work, I can understand why we would set up a life like this. I realize that my rest and recreation life is coming up, and I look forward to it. In my case, I hope sooner rather than later.

Lost in the paths

Everyone has met those poor souls "lost in" the paths. When I refer to it as "lost in" instead of "lost on" the path, I do literally mean "in." When we are lost on the path, there is always a chance that we can find a way out because we are moving ahead. However, "lost in" means we can't find our way out, even with help. Whenever I see these lost souls, I see them as wandering the paths, unable to find their way out of the maze. Getting lost like this signifies serious emotional and psychological problems. Nevertheless, once lost, even the helpful advice of others can't assist them in making it through the maze.

Recently, I attended a very sad funeral of a young father who had become addicted to alcohol and died as a result. There were about three hundred people at the funeral and during his short life not one of these people had been able to help him find his way out of his maze. During these times Spirit will also send help, and even then many people can't find their way onto one of their chosen paths. They spend their last years circling the space and see no way out. Eventually, they spiral out of human life and cross over to the other side. Of course, once healing is given the rehabilitation work commences, and their soul can access the help it requires.

Many people suicide when lost in the paths. It is as if there is no road for them to travel on, so they go "home" to find their peace. Some choose to suicide slowly by living self-destructive lifestyles and ending their lives sooner than necessary. I find it so sad to witness. For them, there is nowhere to go, but home to their God.

Some of us have been there, lost in the paths. However, we made our way back onto some path and could move ahead. Our "missing" time was temporary, and like a blimp in universal time. For others, the outcome was dire.

Never judge others lost in the wilderness, for they are still of the Light and will return to be as one again. It is an unspoken hazard of living in our dimension. Perhaps with this knowledge you can simply help a lost person understand what is happening to them and guide them onto a path, any path, to avert the inevitable.

Being on our designated path or paths is better than wandering the maze. Send light and guidance to those lost souls who find themselves in this unfortunate predicament. If you find yourself there, recognize it and make the necessary changes. Help is always available. You just have to be willing to receive it. Remember, all is possible in the world of Spirit.

Meeting others on the path

In each life, we will be destined to meet certain people. These people will be there, whichever path we opt for. They act as our teachers, here to help us address and work through issues. Not all the people we meet are easily loved. Some of our best teachers may be those we dislike.

The most important people connections for this life need to be able to cross all the paths we choose. So for us to meet them on all paths means their placement is crucial. In general, they are mostly given places in our family, the area we live in or are placed in schools or our work places. Within the family unit, the father, mother and siblings are regularly our greatest teachers. What a surprise!

There are groups of people we will meet on all the paths. These soul groups are there to achieve a particular outcome or for work purposes. These will be groups of people who will choose to re-unite and, through the connection, be teachers for one another.

Destiny determines that we are stuck with them. Before we came to earth, we chose who to be with. I sometimes make a joke about it. Next time I am definitely going to choose fewer challenging individuals to spend my life with. Sure, there were lots of lessons to learn; nevertheless, I picked some tough ones this time. Nonetheless, destined to be together does not mean forever, thank goodness. In my understanding, once the lesson is complete you can choose to part.

Therefore, we have our basic group, and then the other ones on the other paths. If we are supposed to be with someone in this life, it will happen. In that situation, the person will be popping up on every path, so we won't miss them. Besides our basic group, there will be other souls to meet along the various paths. If you choose path two, for example, you will not meet the same people on path four. This has all been factored in before we arrived on earth and each path will bring up unique contacts who will add to our growth.

We are always given free will. Even when we may be destined to meet, it does not mean we have no choice. Often, with the basic group, we may spend more or less time learning from them. It will always be up to us how far we take it. People come into our life for a reason. Whether we embrace the learning around it becomes our choice.

You have set up your own life. Destiny just helps to set the scene and where you decide to go from there determines your future.

Lighting the paths

Knowing we all have these path choices is empowering, especially when we can still retain our free will. However, having choices can complicate life. When we are sure of which path to follow, we have direction and purpose. Then we can steam ahead and be confident that we are heading in the direction we want to go.

The problem arises when we can't decide which way to go. We have all reached the crossroads, trying to work out the right road to take. It is a common human condition. At these times, you can feel confused and be fearful of making a mistake knowing that going a particular way can change your life forever. We struggle with the lack of direction, and as a consequence we can feel stuck. Often all we need to do is to wait and soon the answer presents, and before we know it we are off on our way.

Still, if you receive no sense of direction, there is no need to despair for there is a spiritual solution you may be able to use. One day I just woke up knowing the solution to this dilemma. I was surprised because it was so simple and clear. To begin with you have to recognize that we are all made of light. Each one of us is a soul existing in a human body. Now our soul knows what we have planned for this life, it's our human that gets lost. I discovered the answer lies in connecting into our soul, our light body and the answer is to use the light to make the connection.

In my vision, I was shown how we can light our own path and the path of others. It is easy. To begin with, visualize your best path for this place and time. Next, you light the path. You can send light to the path or as I did, visualize candles along the sides of the path. In my case, I also visualized light being laid down on the actual path. As I could not see the end of the path, I lit it as far as I could. When I looked down the path it was bright and full of light. The light was along both sides and stretched out ahead.

Now my path was full of light, all I had to do was tell my soul body to follow the light. Our souls always work toward the Light, so I knew in time my soul would follow the lighted path, and eventually my human would know where to go. I did not worry about where or when I would walk it. I trusted that as long as I followed the light it would give me my best outcome.

Lighting my own path had another outcome. I stopped stressing. I knew the light would assist me in being guided to my own truth. As I lit the path, I consciously connected to the light. In doing so, I was joined energetically to the light. By giving over to Spirit and surrendering, I knew I would be protected and helped.

After exploring this technique with my own path, I began to light the path of others. Of course, it was done with love and the person's choice to receive it or not. Don't light a path you want for them, rather light the path chosen for their greatest good. Lighting another's path in this way is a loving and generous act. I rarely tell others the spiritual work I send. I do it with much love and always with respect for the choices they ultimately make. Remember, we are here to help and support one another; therefore, using the light is one powerful way to do this.

Before we were born, we all knew the paths we wished to take, the roads of the greatest purpose and growth. Once here it gets confusing, and at times we don't know which way to go. Fear and doubt overtake our inner guidance, and our spiritual antennae can wobble and feel unreliable. On earth, you can't always see the bigger picture.

By lighting the paths, we can use the light to guide us back onto our path. Just be patient and keep lighting those paths and by connecting into your soul you will find your way.

Trouble lighting other's paths

An interesting part of lighting the paths is the problems we can experience when trying to place the light. With some people, the paths I lit were easy. The long stretch of light I visualized to resurface the path went on without difficulty, and the entire process was quick. With other people, lighting their paths was hard work. Although I was sending light to their best path, it remained dim. In a few cases the light I sent would not attach to the path. Even the candles I had visualized were not lighting properly. It was like trying to light wet wood. In another scenario, I lit someone's path, but the whole path dimmed down and went out slowly.

I mention this phenomenon because you could have trouble too. Not all want to follow their path. I realized that on some level, they did not want the lighted path. They were happy to be exactly where they were, even if they said otherwise. Don't be surprised if you encounter these outcomes because some people will even reject the Light. I believe that in rejecting the Light, we reject our true self.

For others, their path has already been chosen. In a sense there is no way back. They are too far down the track to change course, and that path now maps their future. One reason this happens is if the person is going to die soon. It is then that the path may not be altered, for it is in higher hands, so to speak. Although the light we send can help with the crossing, it does not alter the direction. It is their final path before they pass.

Lighting the path is soul work at the highest level, as we will be connecting our soul to their soul. Ultimately, in these situations their soul always has the last say. Energetic work may not be manifest here, but know that our action of love is always registered above. We might want the best for others, but until they want the best for themselves, their ability to receive is compromised. Once we accept this reality it all makes sense.

Blocks to the paths

Choosing a higher path can bring up emotions, so it is important to be aware of this and be willing to move ahead. Don't let your inner conflict stop you. By wrestling our demons and letting go of our anger, hurt or fear, we will be able to remove the emotional block and light our own path.

Intuitively, we all know the emotions that are getting in the way of our progress. We all feel the fear, doubt, anger and frustration. Sometimes the sadness and hurt make movement ahead hard. This knowledge can be a powerful gift for us. For in knowing the emotion we can work at facing it and letting it go. Then our path becomes open and everything in our world can advance.

We are feeling beings. All is emotion on this plane, but that does not mean we can't address our issues and be free of them. Once we lose one emotion another may surface. So all we do is feel it and kiss it goodbye. Fear especially paralyses us all at times. Therefore, without its constricting influence we can move up to the next path of learning.

In lighting another's path be realistic. If they have an emotional block the light might not take. That's okay. Here on earth everyone has choices and their choice might be to sit with the emotion for a time or forever. Blocks are a real issue, particularly when we want to move up to our next path, or we reach a fork in the road. Just being aware of them might be all that is necessary for us to shift them.

Lessons on the paths

On the paths, we will need to repeat certain lessons over and over again. Very often, it may be with the same person. Sometimes the person changes, while the lesson remains the same. Once the lesson is learnt the person or persons may move out of our life. Life as a human is all about the lessons. We came as spiritual beings to live in the material and physical world to broaden our experiences. There are pain and loss. Life on earth is a struggle in comparison to other dimensions, and all who come are strong spirits.

Even though you may have the same lesson on different levels, this should still be seen as moving ahead. As I move through the repeat lesson, I know I am experiencing more soul growth. In this life, I chose to learn the various kinds of the same lesson. For example, I have had many lessons to do with patience. These days I don't get disheartened when a similar lesson pops up again. The sooner we can understand the lessons we have set up for ourselves, the quicker we can get on with other work.

People complain when their lives don't go according to plan. They believe the universe is against them. This is not the case. We agreed to work through many difficult lessons in this life. Some people opted for more than they should have. Their lives can be filled with many ups and downs. On the other side, it all seemed so easy, like deciding to get fit while lying on the couch. The earth reality is very different.

If we are opting for spiritual advancement it is going to be challenging. The lessons will be harder and layered. We may sort an issue out on one level, only to be presented with it on another.

In some lives, we opt to learn how others experience the world and may choose to have a serious illness or debilitating disease. There are many advanced beings living in terrible physical bodies in an attempt to gain understanding. Some people choose to have these illnesses in an attempt to help in the advancement of science. A popular wheelchair bound celebrity was such a soul. His plight helped to further research into paralysis. He championed the cause and made great progress in the field. Once his part was done here on earth, he could return to the other side. No healing in this world could have cured him. His gift to the world was his illness, and in a sense he lit the path for others.

On a personal level, he could comprehend the restriction of his illness and find unknown strength within himself. Many times great souls do their work in this medium, as shining examples to others. It is said that it is not that we fall, but whether we can stand up again that matters. That is what takes courage and builds the soul.

In these situations, other people often agree to come on the journey and support us. It is a mutual, karmic agreement. There is much learning for the support team as well. Soul groups like this can do much to further scientific discoveries for other similarly afflicted persons.

When the person dies, their families continue working for the cause. In human terms this can take the form of appeals, charity work and research. Those left behind know the work has to be done. It becomes their mission and they apply themselves wholeheartedly. Often, even if they are not consciously on the spiritual path, they will unabashedly tell others that the deceased is helping them from above.

We aren't here only to buy cars and put on makeup. Soul growth and learning about the human condition are why we are on earth. We have come to expand our consciousness, balance karma and serve the planet. Many enlightened souls are here at this time to help the planet evolve. They are also dealing with their own evolvement on a personal level. We are all mini versions of the world, with all of its joy, pain, fear and anger. When we all personally take up the challenge, clear our aura and raise our vibration, the world moves with us.

The turmoil in our world is reflected by the inner turmoil we all feel. We live in a sea of energy. Everything is interconnected, as no person is an island. The internal work we do on ourselves contributes to and affects the energy of our world. So as we cleanse ourselves, so the earth is cleansed. More and more people are coming to an understanding of the Oneness that we exist in. No one is alone, for we all change the world by our very existence.

Mother Earth is us, and we are a part of her.

Karmic Healing

*Listen to the wisdom of your soul for your existence here is as
a twinkling in time and space. Within, you hold eons
of knowledge and the key to the universe.*

Karma

Karma is an interesting area. The concept has various meanings to different people and cultures. Generally, I suspect karma has been given quite a negative spin. We have been taught it is an unavoidable punishment, an outcome in which we have very little control. On a human level, karma is presented as a foregone conclusion. It is believed that karma is karma, and whatever we do it remains.

From a soul level, it looks different. In the Garden of Remembrance, we agreed to the amount and way in which we would balance our karma. Our soul decided the karma we wished to work through.

Karma is not a punishment; it's an opportunity for growth. Life on earth is like being in a play, and we play the various parts in order to learn. Once we see karma in this way, it becomes a beneficial experience.

Karma allows us to work things out and in the process balance, our lives. For example, perhaps someone supported us in a previous life, and now we have the chance to repay the debt. In this case, it is not a punishment. I had one friend who knew she was paying back her karmic debt to me. In another life, she was told by Spirit that I had sacrificed my life for her. Now, in this life, she helped me through a difficult, dark time.

The karmic tie is held only until the agreed debt is balanced. After that the relationship dissolves and both parties move on. We can all recognize these karmic debt alliances. As the balance closes, we can feel the shift happening. We all know it's done now, and we are free to go our separate ways.

Often karmic relationships are not like our normal ones. The people are not our usual type of friends. Our human backgrounds might be very different and many of our thought processes can vary. Many may question why they are with a particular person. That can be a sign of a karmic partnership. I have been in these partnerships and wondered why, but now I understand. Usually there is a power imbalance in the relationship and while we are burning our karma it is tolerated.

However, once the karma is paid, we know we can step away. Our soul recognizes the karma is finished. I find that towards the end of a relationship, the other person feels the separation and may try to hold on. Nevertheless, if karmic bonds are all that are keeping us together then once they are gone nothing much is left. This can be a hard truth. Unfortunately, if we try to continue the relationship it can become an unhealthy choice.

Karma and fate

Karma and fate are extrinsically linked, and if there are lessons to be learned or karma to be settled fate will prevail. There are times when karma wins and no amount of pleading or healing can alter the outcome. Over my time working in the spiritual domain I have come to accept when some things are ordained. There are times I would want to send healing to help someone get over an illness or alleviate their suffering, and I would get the message that it was their chosen lesson, their karmic fate.

A young man who had suffered a serious injury comes to mind. Initially, I wanted to go into the hospital and give him healing. I also wanted to send him absent healing. However, my guardians informed me that he needed to experience this for he had chosen this karma. He would be paralyzed for life. It had been agreed to by him as a way to burn off his own karma and the karma of those around him, and any interference from me would be blocked. In this case, I sent him and his family love and light. I understood it had to be this way.

Even though I respected the whole process, I found it sad. Some karmic situations are fate. They are fated to happen whether we like it or not. We set them up to give us opportunities to grow and learn important lessons. How we deal with them is our lesson. Maybe, if in other lives, we have been less than generous with others; it may be our fate to walk in their shoes. Perhaps someone who showed cruelty to a person living a disadvantaged life may reincarnate into a similar life. It will be karma they earned through their actions.

Understanding the way in which karma and fate works can provide us with clarity about the whole process.

Past-life karma

Our life on earth will contain many karmic relationships and lessons, and we will be drawn back to people we have been with before. When we are reunited in this life we will continue where we left off in our previous life. Essentially, a karmic union has a strong feeling of familiarity. We may have been with this soul for several lifetimes and there may be much karma between us. Maybe our karma is to refuse to be controlled this time, or perhaps we have to relinquish our power in this life. The imbalances in these relationships will be obvious to everyone else, while we may take longer to work it out.

Another kind of karma can occur which I call "reunion karma." In previous lives, we may have not been together for as long as we had hoped. Perhaps we became separated by circumstances beyond our control, or one of us died too early to work through our karma. In these circumstances people decide to come back again and finish the uncompleted life together in another time and space. Soul mates generally choose this option. In this way, the lost time can be made up again.

If we are in this kind of karmic relationship, abandonment issues may surface. Be aware it is just the past knocking at the door, a vague fear in our soul memory, and does not signify a loss in this life.

Sacred karmic debt

This is a very powerful type of karma. Sacred karmic debt means we agree to a huge karmic undertaking. The reason I call it sacred is because it is working in the sacred space of the spiritual world.

Karma is fairly easy to do. We may not like doing it, but there is an acceptance and a knowing. With sacred karmic debt, the outlay is enormous and quite daunting, especially from a human perspective. The debts to be paid are so big that during our normal human life, we wouldn't contemplate paying them.

A few years ago I was involved in a sacred debt situation with some old friends. They were pensioners who had an ill daughter living in another city. The mother had terminal cancer and wanted to die in peace knowing that her daughter had a roof over her head. In one of our visits, she asked us to buy a house for her daughter to live in. In that defining moment, Ray and I knew we had to do this and simply agreed. Of course, from a human point of view it seemed like a crazy idea. We were living on one full wage and my small earning, whilst trying to raise three boys. However, Ray and I were okay with the arrangement as it felt strangely right. In time, the mother and daughter passed away, and the house became ours. In addition, as part of the contract, we have taken our bereaved friend under our wings. On a soul level, we know it is what his wife would have wanted, and we know we are paying back a special sacred karma.

I include this example to help explain a sacred contract. We will recognize it by the ease with which we acquiesce. When asked to buy a house for another person most would run away, but we understood it had to be done and went about purchasing it. Our last part of the sacred debt was taking loving care of our widowed friend.

Although the stories will vary, they will achieve the same outcome. Sacred karma is a special kind of bond, which is planned before we arrive and requires a great deal of trust between the two parties. In a sense, it is an act of sacred trust between souls.

Sacred karma is truly working on the highest level one can.

Burning karmic debt

If karmic debt is interesting, burning karma is even more fascinating. People aren't aware that the amount of karma we burn is in our own hands. We can burn off more karma on our earth plane than we realize, and in doing so, will accelerate our own spiritual progress. Burning karma means doing the work needed to complete and erase the debt. By burning the karma in this life, it is not necessary to come back and settle the debt in another life. Although it can be harder to work on some spiritual aspects here in the denseness of earth, the rewards are greater.

I believe that whenever we can't, or won't forgive, the karma may remain. The "unforgiveness" becomes like a tie between you and the others. This tie can span lifetimes. In some cases, not forgiving holds the karma in place. In our society, we are encouraged to think that not forgiving another person is quite okay. However, not forgiving keeps the karma flame burning bright.

In my experience, some of the greatest karma that can be burned comes from that one act, the act of forgiveness. Forgiving is difficult, even impossible for some individuals. Be that as it may, in forgiving the person or persons the karma can finally be over. I believe that until we can release all the anger and hurt that are keeping the "unforgiveness" in place, we can't move on.

It has occurred to me that by not forgiving, we continue to be connected energetically to the relationship or situation. In this way, the issue stays in our life, and if we don't let go, we won't move on.

People aren't always aware that we can also burn karma with those who have passed. By forgiving those already on the other side, we don't have to wait until we cross over. This has a dualistic benefit as both parties can move on.

Another common area where karma exists is in power situations. For the karma to be burned, a balancing of power needs to be achieved. Once the power imbalance is righted, each person can stand on their own feet and make their own choices. Often, after this karma is burned, the relationship finishes and each party is free to move ahead to deal with the next lesson.

An interesting kind of karma burning involves burning good karma. In my life, I have found doing this means you do good even when the person or situation does not really deserve it. In using the term "not deserve it" I am coming from a more human perspective. Burning good karma is being kind, generous and loving to those whom we think don't deserve it. In a spiritual sense, it means working on a higher, soul level.

Burning good karma has very few obvious rewards on earth, but it is a higher way to work. I think it's when our human does not get to scream, rant and rave when it wants. Instead, we bow to a higher power and choose to be loving. For this karma to be burnt properly we have to be sincere in our intention. We can't be just fake.

Over the years, I have worked on burning good karma. In some way it did feel better than being my human self, and I think it taught me to be more at peace with others and their choices.

Karma across the dimensions

An unusual balancing of karma can happen from one dimension to the other which I refer to as "dimensional burn-off." Sometimes certain people die before karma can be settled. Maybe, they were supposed to pay it back. However, when the situation arose, they chose not to deliver and subsequently ran out of time. These karmic debts don't just go away because one person dies. I believe that even in death karmic debt remains. Once people cross over to the other side, they can see their former life very clearly. It is from this dimension that they may choose to pay back their debt. There are many spiritual beings trying to pay their debts to us on the earth plane. They may be trying to help us financially by working their magic, so that our life is made better. At times we may have sensed them trying to help us.

In spite of this, there is an important spiritual truth that we need to be aware of. If we have karmic debt with another, and they die before it is settled, the debt remains. In future lives, it will return to be resolved. The implications are enormous. Both parties will have to address the karma again until it is balanced. It could take many lives before resolution is reached. However, this process can be short-circuited. Just because we are on earth and the person who has crossed over is in another dimension does not preclude resolution, as long as we allow the karma to be settled.

It is beneficial for the deceased to be given a chance to pay the karma by actively assisting the person living. It aids in their spiritual growth. Nevertheless, to be effective, the help has to be received by the living party.

I think that is a great idea, but it can be blocked by us. We all have the capacity to block energetic help for we have free will on earth. Our anger, hurt and disappointment with the deceased can be so strong that the person wishing to send help from the other side cannot reach us. If a soul decides to make amends, but the human involved is unwilling to receive assistance, then only so much can be done.

This is where you come in. If you sense the deceased around, and don't let them help, the debt remains. It is in your and their best interest to allow the help to be received. By doing so, you assist in their healing and allow the debt to clear. It can be hard to let in help from someone who has hurt you. Our human side holds grudges and resentment. Try to keep in mind that on a spiritual basis, it is an extremely evolved kind of karma burning. I consider it to be a unique form of forgiveness that transcends time and space.

It takes great courage and strength to settle karma in this manner. Spiritually, we can make huge growth when we allow healing of this kind to occur.

There is another aspect to dimensional karma clearing. Once the karma is burned, the deceased can move on. Often we can hold up the progress of others on the spiritual plane by not allowing them to rectify a situation that they are held responsible for.

Our life is also improved, for in the balancing of karma we can set off with less baggage, and our time and energy can be utilized in more productive ways.

Opportunities to balance karma

Many humans avoid doing the karmic lessons they set out for themselves. All of us have been avoiders in some way or another. On a spiritual level, some of us are given another chance to deal with the unresolved karma. In these cases, we will meet the persons involved again and be presented with an opportunity for resolution.

I know when this happens, and you probably know too. It goes like this. You are reconnected again and the person is faced with another chance to rectify the karma, and you are willing to give them that opportunity. On a soul level, and maybe human level, everyone knows what it is about. Even when nothing is said, we all know what is supposed to happen.

I find these situations stressful because I recognize, there is a grand plan at work. I know the other person can either choose to step forward or not. In these scenarios, I have little input in the outcome, for they are the ones running from their karmic lesson. It's not about me this time because I have already done my part.

We all have been blessed with free will, and this relates to karmic learning too. We choose when, and if we want to do the karmic time, but no one can make us do it. It is totally up to us, the individual. Regrettably, humans normally take the path of least resistance. So don't be surprised to see others run from these new opportunities, for even when they are given extra time and another chance to resolve an issue, many will choose the easy way and not do it. I have seen these chances come up for others and due to their stubbornness or unwillingness to take responsibility, watched them walk away. However, karma not burned remains, so I know in another place and time it will have to be faced.

You can't be the karma police, although sorting it out might involve you. Ultimately, there is little you can do. Once they decide to shut the door, everyone will have to wait for the next opportunity to present.

Continue to work on your own growth and let it be.

Karma lessons repeating

There are some lessons we have decided to learn in a particular lifetime. Everyone has watched, and maybe they have been part of this process, when the same karmic lessons keep happening until we get it. It reminds me of the movie "Groundhog Day" when every day was like the one before until the main character learned the lesson. I call these repeat lessons.

Repeat karma becomes the same lesson about a particular thing, only in slightly different guises, over and over until we work through the karmic lesson. For some poor souls, I think

Spiritual Answers to Guide Your Life

that never happens in one lifetime. Mostly, it will be a lesson in something like power or unconditional love. As a rule we will keep attracting the same basic situation.

In our lives, we know when someone is doing repeat karma. These are the people who are going out with the loser guy. It is always the same guy, only with another name. The person keeps doing the same boring lesson repeatedly. From a karma perspective, they aren't getting it. The unlearned karma moves on to the next relationship. It is tedious to watch it happening time and time again. It is quite tedious to be the one doing the same thing repeatedly.

The karma is generally cleared once we realize what our lesson is. Many times it is about finally picking up our power with the other person, or maybe learning forgiveness and tolerance. We can balance the karma in most relationships, and once balanced we can move on to the next part.

However, if we find ourselves constantly attracting the same type of people or situation, we need to examine ourselves to discover the reason. This may provide us with the lesson we are to learn.

I had issues with power, so I kept getting into situations with power people and manipulators. No sooner would I think I had sorted it all out, when the next person would turn up. It was interesting because as I worked my way through the lesson, I noticed that these people were becoming more difficult to recognize. It was as if Spirit sent me a power person in various disguises to see how long it would take for me to work it out. I can tell you I was pretty blind to some people along the path.

Soon I found that once I began to work on my own power issues, the repeating lesson changed. Still, it took many years and several karmic lessons before I began to recognize why the same situation kept popping up.

Remember, if we don't deal with the karma in one relationship, another one replaces it. It is the same karmic lesson, only with another person.

Karmic care of others

As mentioned before, there is a strong link between karma and caring for another person. It is very common for this situation to occur. If you look around in your own world you will see it happening. Without fail, the carers involved just "know" they have to do the work and possibly be there until the person they are caring for crosses over. Even if they wish to go, they won't. The carer might whine and complain, yet they always stay. In these cases, the karmic memory is so strong it can't be ignored. Against all the odds, and sometimes much family opposition, they persevere. This kind of karmic debt goes way past the normal care given and can last for decades.

In the Garden of Remembrance, these carers would have agreed to pay back their karma in this manner. Once on earth, at the appropriate time, the karma plays out. One of my friends knew she had to nurse her mother. It took years and over time she became more and more exhausted. However, her deep sense of duty enabled her finally to pay her karma. Perhaps in a former life her mother had done much for her and so in this way she could balance the books. In this case, it was done with much love and patience.

There is another form of karmic debt. At times, if we have treated someone very badly we might have to experience how it feels from the other person's perspective. We could find ourselves caring for a handicapped person or an invalid or being born with some infirmity. Not all of these situations are karmic, but many can be.

Always remember, you and your guardians both agreed to this on the other side. No one made you do it and working through your karma with love and light undoubtedly lightens the load. It means more karma can be burned in this life, which can only be a good thing.

There is much knowledge to be gained from our most challenging lives, so try to see karmic debt as a source of learning.

Karmic poverty

Some of us choose lives of poverty. I hear you groaning and wondering why. There are those who believe we can alter these outcomes with positive affirmations, and in normal circumstances this can work. However, when it comes to poverty karma nothing will alter it, for this plight has been chosen to burn one's karma.

In some cases, you may be poor this time after having lived excesses in past lives. We have all met these princes and princesses from previous lives, struggling with their lack of money in this life. You might have chosen to learn about poverty by immersing yourself in the experience, for there are many insights to be learned in this state. Frequently, the most significant things in life become clearer, like the importance of good health, love and the acquisition of knowledge.

Karmic poverty can be manifest when we lose large quantities of money. Perhaps in other lives we were wealthy, so this time we experience bankruptcy or lose money unexpectedly. I was given this lesson when buying tickets for an overseas trip. The first company I chose to deal with was too slow, and so I went to another travel agent. My decision was guided by following my psychic feelings. Within weeks the second company went into liquidation. The day the phone call came through remains vivid. As the travel agent told me I had lost all of my money, I felt my stomach drop. It was a feeling I will never forget. After the initial shock, I asked my guardians why I had been drawn to change travel agents and lose all the money. I was informed it was to teach me about the emotions involved when losing money. Obviously, it was my karmic lesson.

Another interesting karmic lesson regarding money concerns the sharing of wealth. Certain individuals come into massive amounts of money. They have wealth we only dream of. Part of their karma may be to use the money for the greater good of others. If they recognize their responsibility, they will use the money to set up charities, foundations, etc. Considering the wealth abounding in our world it seems clear that many are not burning much karma. I think if we have come to earth to do good work and don't do it, it can be like a boomerang coming back and hitting you in the head. We have all seen others falling off their money pile. In these cases, it was the result of their actions, greed and selfishness that eventually led to their downfall. Being rich can bring with it responsibility, and I wish more people would realize this spiritual truth.

Our society is so hung up on money that it keeps many of us slaves to its power. Still, we measure success by the size of our wallet. It's strange, because our most influential world leaders had little money. Jesus, Buddha and Gandhi all changed the lives of millions, and yet owned very little.

Karma affecting having children

In this section I want to put forward a strange karmic lesson concerning having children. There are some situations where due to past lives, some people have trouble conceiving.

Over the years, I have come across an unusual karmic balancing. A couple I was working with was having difficulty conceiving. What had happened in a previous life was influencing this one. I was informed that in a past life, she had been a very poor parent and had incurred karma. That meant that she was unable to have children easily. So in this life all kinds of difficulties arose, and in the process, she learnt to appreciate the special gift that children are.

Of course, once this form of karma is balanced children can still arrive.

I find this section hard to write about. It is not my intention to put any blame or guilt on those who have trouble conceiving. I only write about this to inform you of another aspect of karma.

Karmic stagnation

Karmic stagnation occurs when one or the other party does not move on. Ideally, the karma needs to be sorted, and then each moves on. The aim of a karmic partnership is to achieve completion, not to last forever. By holding on, stagnation happens and future plans can get held up. Our society encourages us to be nice to everyone. Having lots of friends and keeping them is seen as the best outcome. Issues of loyalty and being a good friend are seen as favorable attributes.

However, if we have already agreed to come together and then move on, different attitudes need to be in place. Staying in the same space can block everyone's progress. I had plenty of trouble disconnecting on a human level with a number of people because, in my mind friends should be there through thick and thin. My background had taught me that a good friend stayed to the end. Now I was finding my reality was different. I would begin to realize that the relationship was coming to an end, even when I did not want it to be so. In my soul, I knew it was over; the karma was complete. There are those souls we choose to be with forever, some for a while and others until the lesson is learned or completed.

We are not deserting them. We are setting them free once the karmic account is balanced.

Frequently, we can overstay, so knowing when it is over is very important. Many know, but stay regardless. In their heart, they know what should be happening, but they block it. Stagnation like this is detrimental to all concerned. Timing is everything on the earth plane, because we exist in a linear world.

At this time in our evolution, we can burn much karma and move through at an accelerated rate. The energy at this time allows it. I urge everyone to take advantage of this era, and move through and allow others to do, likewise.

It's the human in us who wants to stay, while the soul wants to fly. Be true to yourself and listen to your inner guidance.

Fragmented karma

People sense when the karma is not completely over, even if both parties have moved on. Karma can be split like this, with each person sensing it is not quite finished. Fragmented karma is common. In our human world, we have to construct the situations in which the karma can be sorted. Occasionally,

Spiritual Answers to Guide Your Life

we clear a certain amount at one time, and then deal with the leftover later. It is not unusual for karma to have sections and that is why a broken relationship can come together again. On the second or third time around the residual karma is balanced. This is why I think some karma takes longer to be settled.

If we are required to go back and redo a section, we should not be angry with ourselves, as it needs to be done. It will feel unlike doing the first part, where we would have let it go, moved on, and thought it was complete. We are not really returning to the whole relationship, for mostly it is just an adjustment, to complete or settle it. I have experienced these return karmic visits. They can feel weird and surreal, like you are in a play. It is as though the last part needs a final tweak, and then it's complete. However, on a human level the experience can feel quite uncomfortable.

Fragmented karma works like this. You may find yourself accidentally bumping into the "karma" people in order to sort out another section. In another scenario, you will have an overwhelming urge to phone the person and speak a truth, or settle a grey area. I always feel like I am on auto-pilot when this happens. Maybe that's because the exchange is more on a soul level, even though it is occurring in a human dimension.

See these exchanges as balancing the karma, an opportunity for each soul to complete the work. Fragmented karma gives us the opportunity to settle things once and for all, and allows everyone to move ahead.

Quickening karma

Our world is vibrating faster and faster, and I believe the speed at which karma can occur is also being affected.

We live in the instant world, with everything "coming back at us instantly," so to speak. The same thing is happening with karma. I call it quickening karma, and I found it works differently to some karma as we know it.

With quickening karma every action has an instant reaction. For example, if you say something unkind, the karma can come back at you within minutes or hours. I know someone who had experienced lots of dental problems. She had broken a couple of teeth in the last year. Her husband on hearing this began a tirade telling her to take better care of her teeth. He reminded her how expensive it was becoming for the rest of their family. That evening the husband broke a tooth. He was experiencing quickening karma.

There are signs everywhere of quickening karma. Talking unkindly or being discourteous to someone can precipitate quickening karma. Even being very angry and sending them bad vibes can easily result in you wearing the karma too, so be careful. I tend to think being involved in road rage is a physical manifestation of this form of karma in action.

Quickening karma is happening more and more because every aspect of our life on earth is speeding up. Our understanding of its effect on our daily lives will allow us to make informed choices about living in love and peace.

Understanding our Past Lives

*Look for the lesson for you in all situations
for it is a vehicle for your learning.*

Past lives

We are all of our past lives. They are encoded in our aura and define us; therefore, knowing about these lives can enrich this life. When I began this work, I was not terribly interested in past lives. Naively, I thought they were all about the past and had little impact on my present life. How wrong I was!

Over the years, I began to recognize the enormous wealth of information stored in those lifetimes. Past lives are like the keys to our soul, opening doorways to untapped gifts, experiences and occupations. Knowledge of even one life can shine the light on aspects of us that we have not yet accessed. Everyone will have numerous past lives to draw on. In human terms, there are some souls who have spent hundreds of lives on earth, while others have spent countless lives in other dimensions.

I remember going to a herbalist who had a psychic gift. At the end of the session, he asked me if I looked at the stars. He then continued to tell me that my soul seed originated in the constellation of Orion's Belt. At that time, I had not embarked upon my healing path, and I must admit it sounded weird to me. These days I am grateful for his insights, and it now makes perfect sense to me.

It's an interesting concept to imagine we aren't all from here. The reality is that just because we live as "Bob" in this life, it doesn't mean we haven't come from other galaxies. I know this information is like science fiction for some people, but as we vibrate faster, it will all seem like common knowledge to us.

People can struggle with the concept of living past lives in other places besides earth. We have been taught earth is the centre of the universe. In this century, there are many from other galaxies and worlds living on earth. Although I have not seen them in the normal sense of seeing, I feel their presence. A few of my friends are very aware of their existence and can describe them in detail. One psychic friend has a family of blue visitors, while another has a group of very tall, almost opaque bluish beings near her. My friends who see these visitors feel unphased by the whole thing.

Lots of beings are on earth to help. They take different forms. Some can be seen by others, while some are actually here in a human form. Have you ever thought you could have been in other dimensions? If you are from other worlds the earth can feel unfamiliar. By drawing on your past lives you may be able to remember other realities. When we have had many past lives in other galaxies, we may wonder why people here do what they do, as it might seem strange to us. You can access these past-life existences and use the knowledge in this life. Once you are open to the idea you may have come from another dimension, your soul will be free to let more information flow in.

Of course, our life now is human. However, our soul contains all we have already experienced, so tapping into these past lives will be well worth it.

Past-life illness

Illnesses are regularly rooted in past lives. Unresolved, they will pop up in the next life and, strangely enough the sickness often presents when we are the same age as in the previous past life.

For example, a young man I knew started to have trouble with his right arm about the age of twenty. After some past-life information surfaced, it became obvious he had been handicapped about the same age. In his past life, his right side was crippled, and he walked with uncomfortable braces on his legs and used a stick. Once he reached the same age the handicap memory was triggered. Fortunately, he addressed that life and within the next few months the afflicted arm began to improve. Obviously, he had been carrying around this pain for many lifetimes waiting for an opportunity to release it.

A past-life pain can be triggered when meeting a person from the same past life. Once the connection is made, the past-life illness can come up in this life again. This strange phenomenon happened to someone I know. A friend of mine married, and within years began to experience severe eczema. She could find no reason for it. The eczema lasted throughout the marriage. Eventually, she decided to leave her husband and, miraculously, the condition cleared up, and she has never had it again.

It is important to explore the role past lives can have on your health. Some people can access this information themselves. However, most of us need the help of a gifted psychic.

Fears and phobias from past lives

You can carry these fears and phobias throughout the ages, as they are unresolved soul experiences. I think we carry them through for various reasons. Sudden or traumatic death can trap these emotions in the aura. It is like they are frozen in the aura. Sometimes, when the person dies suddenly or undergoes great trauma, the soul has no time to process the emotions involved. Even though we cross and have an opportunity to heal, elements from the past life can remain.

In some instances, souls come back into their next life too soon. They choose to return before adequate healing has occurred, so they drag their issues in with them again. If we choose to come back too early and don't stay long enough to receive the necessary healing, we can't resolve these issues properly.

In general, we don't return to the earth plane for several lifetimes. Perhaps we decide to visit another dimension to expand ourselves. Without the earth vibration, these fears and phobias can't be addressed. I believe we need to be on earth to work through some of our unfinished business because our earth presents opportunities not available in other spheres.

Another aspect is synchronicity. If we need to work through a fear or phobia with certain people, we might have to wait for many lifetimes before we are all together again. We can have several lives here and "abroad" before we can be in the same place to tackle the fears and phobias.

There are countless types of past-life fears and phobias. I met a lady, who had a terror of birds. She had no memory or insight of the origin of the terror. Even so, her irrational fear had become a constant problem for her in this life, and she was frightened of all birds. As birds are everywhere, her life was a nightmare. When I tuned into one of her past lives with birds, I saw a disturbing scene. I saw her being tied down on a platform on a beach with the birds attacking her for days. She had been killed for some crime in a tribal ritual. By facing her past-life experience, she could process it and let it go. The release could finally be done by the soul.

Water fears feature strongly in past-life phobias. The fear is particularly powerful for the person because it nearly always involves a traumatic death by drowning. A lady who came to me had such a fear of water, especially cold water. By tapping into the past life it became evident she had been crossing a frozen lake when she fell through the ice. Unable to climb out of the water, she slowly froze to death. The person concerned could now understand her phobia and begin to make sense of her world. At last this lady could release this crippling phobia and work towards healing the past.

Past-life information can be accessed by a clear reader or healer. Before you arrive for your session, ask your guardians to relay the necessary information to the reader. If the time is right, you may receive helpful descriptions of the time and events. Some readers literally see the past life like a movie. When I read past lives, I can see it in my head in that way.

If you want to heal a past life ask your guardians to show you how. They can use dreams, visions or relay the information through a movie or book. I have found my reactions to some situations gave me insights. Invariably, when it is a past-life revelation you can get goose-bumps. Goose-bumps are an affirmation that your soul is speaking to you.

Hypnosis and rebirthing, also known as breath work, can uncover fears and phobias. A trained practitioner can take you back to that terrible time. In the here and now, you can safely observe and learn what is hidden from you. Much relevant information can surface using these techniques. Self-hypnosis can work for many people, as well.

The work we do in uncovering our fears and phobias will free us in this life and the ones to come.

Activating gifts and knowledge from past lives

Remembering where we have been in past lives can help us tap into a gift or skill lying dormant in our aura. The aura records everything. In recalling past lives, we can discover vast amounts of "hidden" talents.

Sometimes, we have an inkling of a latent gift. Maybe we have always wanted to sing and been too shy, or there is an artist inside us longing to paint again. You can tell when you have hit on a past-life gift. You will have a feeling of coming home. There may be some fear around learning a new skill, but there is also a sense of peace, like you have done this before. I have noticed that this feeling of familiarity comes frequently with past-life gifts. The first night I returned from my introductory massage lesson, I remember saying to my husband how it felt as though I had done this before. I knew it was not in this life, but my hands remembered the feeling. He too thought the way I was using my hands seemed strangely confident.

I am not saying we will not struggle at times to grasp the skill again and need to hone it. However, the time it takes to regain the skills is always quicker than expected. In time, we will be able to make up for lost ground and further our gift. Once we reach the place we left off in our last life, we will be well on our way.

Timing is everything in reactivating your old gifts. You may reach important times in your life when the gift can be reactivated. Teachers in the required field will arrive, and you will have the time and space to pursue your gift. On a universal level, the scene is set, and you can begin.

The gifts

Where we start with the gift may not be where we finally end up. I began doing massage work. I can now see it was only the beginning of opening my gifts from my past lives. Through massage, I moved into hands on healing, and soon I began to channel and could connect to beings on the other side. These days I am writing books and painting channeled art.

The first opening to one past life may lead directly into another. You cannot always know where one gift begins, and the other ends. I trust that the "upstairs people," as I call them, know best. I ask for my gifts to be used for the greatest good, and in this way I can be sure I am heading in the right direction. The progression from one skill to another can be daunting, but quite exciting. Once one area is mastered another comes into play. Of course, we never have to go ahead, unless we want to. I have found my total trust in Spirit allowed me to be led along safely to the next place.

When I feel unsure, I tap into my feelings. If it feels right I go ahead, if I can't quite decide, I wait and trust guidance will come. Mostly, it is only a timing thing. Maybe we know we need to open the next gift, but the time does not feel right. It is okay to wait.

This is what happened when I was writing these books. I was anxious to complete it, so I wanted to work through the Christmas break. As fate would have it, family concerns and an inability to create any new chapters, meant nothing manifested. Once I got back to work, I realized the break had brought much clarity, and I spent the next few months completely overhauling the books.

Remember, when you are using a gift, be patient and let it evolve naturally.

Untapping old gifts can sometimes present another dilemma. Be aware of hindering your own progress. Once you have mastered a skill, there is a comfort in it, the initial fear has gone, and for the most part, it becomes easy. Letting go and moving into uncharted waters can bring up much fear.

Sometimes, when we have devoted much of our life to a chosen activity, it can be hard to let it go. I struggled when I began to do less healing work, and more writing and painting. A part of me resisted moving on. I loved doing the work and wanted to continue working as a healer/reader. I had fantasized about owning my own healing sanctuary, and was having difficulty letting go of my dream. A good friend helped me see it in another way. She felt that just because we can do something, it does not mean that we have to. It gave me permission to allow myself to acknowledge my gift as a healer/reader and yet be able to expand into other areas. So these days a lot of my time is taken up writing books.

Where we start is rarely where we end up. Don't stunt your own growth by being unwilling to expand into new territory.

There is another aspect to consider. People will want to pigeonhole you. For example, some are unlikely to support your decision to change your course. The people who came to me for massage, readings and healings wanted me to keep doing it. They couldn't understand why I was now writing. Although I knew it was the next gift I had to activate, they wanted me to stay the same. So I suggest that you be strong and follow your intuition.

In the process of remembering past lives and moving ahead, money can become scarce. While your new gift is developing, you may be tempted to go back to old ways. Persevere, because given time your path can also be lined with gold. Remember that all comes to those with faith.

Future lives

I am very curious about future lives. I believe time does not exist in the same way that we have devised it for this

Spiritual Answers to Guide Your Life

human life. The universe operates in a timeless environment so everything can be happening simultaneously. This means all of your lives are happening at the same time. Think of yourself as a multi-storey building with each floor being one of your lives, so that all your lives will be happening in the same block of "time and space."

I know on a soul level that some of the work I have done on myself will affect my future lives, with the clearing and settling of karma directly changing the course of my next lives. When I say next, I can also mean right now, all at the same time.

If time does not exist, I should be able to access past, present and future simultaneously. Now I can work at releasing emotions like anger and fear from the future lives. Wow, what a thought!

Due to my own belief in no time barriers existing, I always include my future lives in my requests. I know that everything I need, I can have now, wherever it is stored, and that I can ask for access to any gifts or skills held in the vaults of my future lives. Who knows what is held there for we know the soul is not held by time or space? Those concepts are a human design. By working in a limitless universe, we can move ahead on all levels.

The future is within our grasp because time really does not exist in the world of Spirit.

Connecting to Guidance

*Sometimes, when we can't see our guardians it is
because they hold us so close. It is then that
their wings encompass our whole being.*

Your guides

Everyone has spiritual guidance with them. However, not everyone is aware of the help at hand, even though Spirit is ever present. Like sentinels, they wait for us to be ready to receive their guidance. As well, you have ancestors with you on earth, nearby to share your daily life. Often, if we are open, they can send us thoughts and ideas. Relatives and friends on the other side are always trying to assist from above. Due to our family connections, they can easily relay information to us. Unfortunately, though, most of the time their efforts go unnoticed.

I know some spirits try to find good partners for their loved ones. I had occasion to give a widower a message from his late wife. She wanted him to know she was bringing a new person into his life. At the time that I spoke to him, he was adamant it was all rubbish, but he did tell me that he remembered a strange dream. In the dream, his wife told him she wanted him to be in a relationship again, as she did not want him to be lonely. She gave him her blessing. Within a couple of years, the lady had arrived, and he was no longer alone. Relatives can do much from the other side.

They can even send us gifts. When my mum died the few jewels she owned were split up. I had always loved her ruby ring. On my mother's death, it was given to my sister. A decade later my mum "sent" me a ruby ring. On my fiftieth birthday, my family gave me a lovely ruby ring. The spiritual world is like that; they see what is in your heart and will try to give it to you. The dimensions make no difference.

Spirit finds ways to reach us. They might whisper in an open ear, and plant the thought. Perhaps I was going to be given something else on my fiftieth birthday, but by Spirit sending the thought a new gift idea was arranged. I am sure there have been times you have wanted to have something, and then suddenly you are given it. It is like someone was reading your deepest thoughts. I thank Spirit when this happens because I understand they are hearing my wishes and prayers.

I believe it is important to appreciate the gifts from Spirit. Orchestrating it from their side can be very hard as they have to sow the seed and then wait for a human to physically do the work.

Getting people to meet can be one of the most challenging ventures for Spirit. Free will can mess it up big time. Spirit may have it all organized, and then one of the parties decides not to go to the arranged meeting place. I wonder if this didn't happen in my life. I knew my husband Ray for years before we came together. When I went here or there he would be at a work function or dance, so we were being placed in the same space waiting for the chance to start our life. Both of us were in relationships with other people. I can imagine Spirit's frustration. Then my partner went off to "find" himself, and as soon as he was gone in popped Ray. The rest is history as they say.

We can ask for spiritual help for ourselves and others. We all basically know this truth. I have found faith strengthens the outcomes because it keeps you listening, even when nothing has manifested. It teaches us to be patient and to understand that many other things can come into play.

It is very important to realize that we only see part of the picture. Spirit can see all. Just because we can't understand why things are happening in an expected way does not mean it is wrong, for often there are bigger outcomes that we are not aware of.

These days I accept their wisdom, and I have discovered that I no longer need clarity or the answer. If it is not forthcoming, I continue to trust that Spirit is privy to more information and that there is a greater plan. We need to have faith that all is taken care of in divine time.

Respecting your guardians

Your guardians operate like your friends. So, remember to be aware of this. Although they have chosen to work with you, they decide how much help is given. They can stand close or watch from afar.

In my life, I have tried to treat them with great respect. Not all people do. It is unwise to curse and get angry with them as they always try to help us, even if we can't see it. Some people become exceedingly nasty to them. I have heard the way they speak about their own guardians. They give them ultimatums and blame them for not giving them this or that. Humans can get very mean when Spirit does not come through as they demand. Humans are by nature power freaks and demanding.

I can't think of a more tedious job than trying to be someone's guide.

When we ask for guidance it comes. The only time it does not is when they stand back. The usual reasons are that we have to learn from the experience, or they are standing back because we are being uncooperative. Most of us are hard to reach, even on a good day and especially when it comes to our own personal issues. I have witnessed some of the most enlightened people being as stubborn as a mule.

Remember, if Spirit stands back, we are always the reason. If we decide to throw a temper tantrum they will step away.

If we decide to do it our own way they literally stand back, thereby allowing us to exercise our free will. On a spiritual level, if we decide to give up doing the spiritual work, the guides who were sent in order to assist us will move on. I know of people who have lost these guides. From a guide's point of view, there is little point in staying when their skills can be used with a more cooperative student.

Guides are a gift. They are not your servants or whipping boys. We all need to understand that love and respect go a long way. Your personal life guardian will stay with you for this life. However, they can choose how much help they try to give and like a good friendship, it can be destroyed by selfish actions.

Never blame your guides. You have manifested your spiritual world. I have seen many frustrated guides shaking their heads in disbelief. When I see them, they are there, but they seem to stand at a distance waiting. These are the life guides. Usually the specialized spiritual helpers are long gone.

Spirit is always there wanting to help. If you feel you could have inadvertently caused your guides to step away, you can ask for them to come back. It will be up to you to mend the connection.

The gatekeeper

One of your guardians will assume the major role of the gatekeeper. It is a role of spiritual protection. Of course, your entire team will work to guide and help you. However, the gatekeeper will communicate directly to you when danger is around. The gatekeeper is your personal spiritual assistant who will help you in daily life and protect you from unwanted spiritual interference.

I was told by Spirit that the gatekeeper has the top position with security. Obviously, we need to have protection from all the things that can go wrong here on earth. Whether it is personal safety when crossing the road or driving down the highway, the gatekeeper will keep guard. We all have had times when we should have been injured, yet by some miracle were safe.

You can ask the gatekeeper of other people to give extra protection to them at times. Recently, one of my sons needed to pick up his new boat. It was a long, winding drive through the mountains and both my husband and I felt uneasy. On the day, I asked his gatekeeper to protect him from any danger. It was strange as he also felt some apprehension, and so he made sure he took his toolkit and spare wheels. On returning home, he rang me. The trip had been safe, except for the fact he had not realized that the trailer wheel bearing had broken, and the wheel had almost seized. How he managed to make the two-hour journey home safely was a miracle! In my heart, I knew his gatekeeper had protected him.

Another situation which can surface is when you could possibly be killed, and it is not your time to die. Then the gatekeeper will protect you, mainly by lifting you out of danger until it passes. How many times have we witnessed horrific accidents and marveled at how the person survived? Well, in spiritual terms, we have the gatekeeper to thank.

There is another way we can be protected. Those of us who are actively engaged in spiritual work can ask our gatekeeper to keep our energy field protected. Our aura can then remain our sacred place. There have been times I felt I needed extra protection. Whenever I sense any psychic attack or spiritual interference I ask my gatekeeper for a wall of energetic protection. In the psychic world, many people are skilled at manipulating energy, and we can be vulnerable to these psychic attacks. These are not honorable practices, still they do occur. Unfortunately, on a human level we can't always be aware of these invasions and that is where the gatekeeper becomes invaluable.

The gatekeeper will be skilled in these areas. Spirit can, likewise, guide you to cleanse your aura, use the sage smudge stick or have a salt bath when your aura has been attacked. This knowledge of when to do this will come directly from the gatekeeper.

The more we become involved in spiritual work, the more important the gatekeeper becomes. As yet we are only aware of one tenth of the energetic exchange occurring on earth. Therefore, all protections are valuable.

Some people prefer to call in archangels for extra help. These beings are from the angelic realm, and they will assist you at any time. I like to use them too. It is an extra choice we have.

Not everyone wants to delve into their spiritual life. Nevertheless, we can send help to them by talking to their gatekeeper. If we feel others need protection, ask their gatekeeper to help. As always, they will decide, but at least they will be given some aid. All of us are powerful souls, and the doorways to spiritual connection are ever open. I have faith that even the most ardent disbelievers can be reached by the gatekeeper.

I honor my gatekeeper and I know if I ask for assistance that it will come. Remember, one can disregard the information, but it won't be beneficial to do so. I have observed people being shown the way to block unwanted psychic activities. However, due to their own stubbornness, they have not done so. As a consequence, the attacks and disturbances continued.

Playing around with psychic situations like these can lead to imbalance and danger, so I advise you to follow the messages you receive.

At times, the gatekeeper may choose to speak through others to relay information to you. These people become the messengers. In my life, they have been family members and close friends. Sometimes, strangers can also be used.

I consider the gatekeeper to be one of the most important guardians you have with you. They rarely change like some of the other guides, and many have been with us several lifetimes. We may have even served them in some lives as their gatekeeper. The gatekeeper is our strongest ally in keeping us safe here and in the psychic realm.

Time as signs of connection

Once you begin to connect with the spiritual realm you may notice an unusual physical sign. You may begin to get certain number patterns coming up. For me, it came up with the time on the clock. Every time I looked to see what the time was it was elevens, twenty twos and thirty threes. I noticed it straight away as it was so consistent. It did not matter whether it was day or night. I could wake in the middle of the night, and it would be two eleven or four twenty two.

It is a sign we are in direct communication with Spirit. Generally, day or night I would greet them when I saw the numbers and acknowledge, they were signing to me. It felt great and very validating to have this tangible sign from the spiritual world.

There was a bonus for me, because when I saw the numbers I knew they were sending me more information. In a sense, it was a spiritual download similar to our way of downloading information via the computer.

Notice your patterns. Whether it is on car number plates or signs, they are your personal "dial-in" to the universe.

During times of spiritual growth, the amount of number sightings can increase dramatically. You might see your numbers countless times within a short time frame and with each sighting your connection to Spirit strengthens. I have noticed that I can have more sightings in times of stress or difficult phases of my life. I think it is Spirit's way of reassuring me of their presence, for although we are never alone, the path can seem lonely and deserted. I find their number flashes comforting and grounding as I know spiritual help is there in a tangible way.

Never compare your numbers with others. My husband gets more double numbers like forty four, fifty five and thirty three. The numbers and where we see them make no difference. All that matters is your acknowledgment of this spiritual connection in your daily life.

These days I greet my guardians and use the number signals as a prompt to speak to them. I give thanks for my blessings and express my gratitude. Every time we contact via the numbers our aura becomes more receptive to carrying the light. It is like we are melding into their auras, and they are melding into ours. The overlap directly strengthens the spiritual body.

These higher beings vibrate in other spheres to us, and I believe when we touch them with our hearts and minds, we also touch their hearts and minds. In this way, the energetic exchange brings us closer to the Oneness, the Light.

Sensing spirits in the house

One of the gifts of being psychic is the ability to sense spirits around you and others. Some psychics virtually see spirits, as if they were here in person, some sense where the energy of the person or animal is located in the room, and others get fleeting glimpses like orbs or moving lights.

Everyone sees with different eyes in a human sense, so why wouldn't we all have different ways of seeing spirits too. Try to be content with the way you see and work on honing your particular gift. I think it is counter-productive to want what others have, especially in this field. Everyone comes from various experiences in other worlds and past lives, and, even if we want to "see" like others it may be impossible, given the various soul lives.

In some cases, if we are not born with the gift it can be given to us. Years ago, I met an old psychic lady who had the gift of seeing spirits. I knew she could see in her mind, and at times, in the real world. As she was ill, I had been guided to visit her and give healing. This went on for several months. Over this time, her age began to affect her, and dementia began to take hold.

On the last visit when I did the healing a wonderful thing happened. While I was working on her, she asked me to stop. Next she touched her forehead and reached over to me and touched my forehead in a symbolic gesture. Even now I still remember her words. She told me she could no longer use this spiritual gift due to her declining health, her gift of seeing spirits, and so her guardians had instructed her to place it upon my brow and in my care. I thanked her, but really had little idea of what had occurred. Over the following months, I began to receive more and more pictures in my head. If a deceased person came to visit, I could see them in my mind and sense where they were standing in the room. When they came a day or two before a reading I would know they were there waiting for their loved one to arrive.

When I worked, I could see how someone's past life looked. The pictures resembled a movie in my mind's eye, and I could describe in detail the clothes worn and places they lived.

If you do not receive a gift you can still ask to ascend in this area. Perhaps you will not be given the gift in the manner I received it, but your gift can increase in some other way, often when you least expect it. A friend who wished to become more spiritually aware saw her first fairy. Few adults see fairies and the nature nymphs, although a lot of children do. It shows that we all have the gift even years after childhood. What an exciting prospect!

Asking guides to talk to each other

There are times when all our attempts to get through to someone seem to no avail. During these times, I resort to asking my guardians to speak to their guardians. Our guides, like us, are in constant communication. It is through them many of our spiritual attempts are facilitated. When we do readings and during channeled healings, they are the connection points relaying the information.

Guardians see all that happen because their view of all situations is vast and clear. While our human desires and prejudices can color how we interpret messages from the other side, the guides see only with a pure intention. These days when I am struggling to deal with a situation, I ask them for help.

For example, if two people are supposed to be together to fulfill their soul purpose, but one party keeps blocking the union it is wise to enlist spiritual help. Once you recognize the problem is too big to surmount in the human world, you can hand it over to their guardians. We all know some things are greater than us, and so by surrendering to Spirit more can be achieved.

I believe that even in your worst moments your guardians can reach you and orchestrate change. People who have attempted suicide, and failed, may know on a deep soul level that their attempts have been foiled. When someone is not supposed to cross to the other side their guardians will intervene. Their guardians will alert the guardians of someone they know and the suicide attempt will, in many cases, be interrupted. At these times, those trying to suicide are found by a family member or friend before serious damage occurs, or miraculously, a visitor arrives at the crucial time and stops the suicide attempt.

In these situations, both sets of guardians are communicating. One signals to the others that outside help is needed and this spiritual message is relayed by the guides to the people concerned resulting in the suicide being avoided.

Even seemingly non spiritual people can be reached in this manner. Although we are here as humans, most of our gut feelings come from the soul. It is our strongest urge, as the soul is the engine that drives the human.

When we request help from guardians, it will be given. Nevertheless, keep in mind that everyone will continue to have free will. Instead of over-riding your decisions, the guardians will try to set up opportunities for different outcomes. In the case of suicide, the person is still allowed to try and suicide, thus respecting their free will. However, Spirit will work at blocking the outcome and in so doing, give the person another chance. I mean if you still want to kill yourself eventually the guardians may stand aside. The reason I mention suicide is because many times it is attempted when people are in a highly emotional state and not thinking straight. Given time, and being in a calmer place emotionally, most people would no longer choose to kill themselves.

The guardians can help with relationships. A few years ago a friend of mine was going out with a younger man with whom she was having a great time. Their connection was strong due to past-life relationships, and he admitted to her that he too was falling in love. At the time they met, he was supposed to marry a bride his mum and dad had chosen for him. It was their family tradition. This time he was supposed to follow his heart and to begin to live his own life, not his parent's. The lesson had been set up earlier in the Garden of Remembrance. However, fear gripped him, and he began to fall back into old patterns, the fear blocking his chance of happiness. He was following his head, not his heart.

In the human world, nothing was working, so the two sets of guardians were called in order to assist them both. Their only chance was asking for higher spiritual help.

Everybody has free will. With these two people, the man chose not to accept the help given by Spirit. He made a decision based on old ways of thinking and fear, but this work from Spirit filters down. Although he chose not to follow his heart this time, he may in the future. When we have hard lessons to learn we can falter several times before we finally break through our fears and blocks.

You can ask for help concerning discord between people. Perhaps there has been a disagreement or issue and separation has occurred. The parties involved may want the relationships back. However, they are unable to find a solution. Their guardians can assist in breaking down the barriers. Spirit can help them to meet accidentally and have another chance for reconciliation. In this scenario, no-one loses face and possible rejection. These unexpected meetings can rekindle relationships.

I have had separations causing pain and sadness. The people concerned are not in my physical world, yet I feel that they are always in my heart and mind. If you wish for another chance to see if it can work ask the guardians to set it up. You might be surprised.

I accept that when soul work is messed up by our human selves, we need to be open to spiritual aid. Our guardians hold all our hopes and dreams in their hands, and are truly coming from a place of love and truth.

If the opportunity is lost, they will know and let it be until another time. Once we have asked for their help, be prepared for the necessary outcome. Know all that could have been done has been done. Remember, humans are stubborn and difficult to reach at times.

In general, when given a difficult spiritual lesson most people will avoid it or only go so far. Don't be too disappointed if your request to Spirit can't be delivered in the here and now. When the outcome is less than desired, know that all has been done with love and hope. Humans can be hard to work with and at times can only put their toes in the water. Very few can jump in and swim to the other side.

Sharing guides

During a healing for someone, I was made aware of the concept of sharing guides. When I was introduced to this concept I was intrigued. The way I understand it is that some souls decide to also have a shared guide or guides in their earth life. For example, I would have the same guide as my husband or child. The guide belongs to us both. It is our guide, not a guide only designated to one person.

Shared guides are a unique occurrence, and are only used between certain people. I don't feel it is a common practice. These types of guides can bi-locate, being in a few places in the same time and space. Therefore, the guide would be with you and the other person simultaneously.

The reason this sharing arrangement is used is to ensure the well-being and support for each person. It is like insurance for when times get hard. Some higher beings have taken on extremely arduous lives to learn from. The toll on them is enormous and consequently, burnout, and accidental death is always a reality. With the extra "shared" guide these incidents can be averted. For example, if one partner became suicidal the guide would alert the other person, and it could be prevented, or if through circumstance one of the people was in danger the shared guide would immediately be aware of it and make the danger known to the other person.

I learned about the existence of these guides when I was working on a suicidal woman. Spirit explained that she and her husband shared a guide to avert any situations in which they could be in danger. This had actually happened recently when her husband "knew" he had to go home and, in doing so, stopped her from dying from an overdose. The shared guide was able to warn him of the imminent danger.

Before we arrive on earth, we can see the pitfalls. Unfortunately, once in human form the soul mission can become very different. When the human goes off the rails, these shared guides can make the difference between life and death. In a way they ensure the individual is protected from themselves and others.

I think shared custody is a valuable spiritual reality. The world of Spirit is an incredible place, and I never cease to be amazed by how wonderful it is.

Asking for specific teaching guides

Another way to accelerate your learning is to ask for specific spiritual teachers to be with you. When I was learning my craft, I wanted healers to help me advance my skills from a spiritual perspective. Intuitively I knew that I could ask them to join me and help in my journey.

In my case, I always knew when a new guide was with me because the way I worked would change, and I could sense the shift in energy. My hands would move differently, and my old way of working would be replaced with other techniques. Generally, before the new teacher began to work with me, I would have a quiet time. There would be a lull in my workload with few people coming to me. During this time, I would feel my aura shifting as I was adjusting my vibrational rate in readiness for the next healing teacher.

While working with your latest teacher you might find yourself drawn to using different essential oils or cultural healing models. With one of my new guides, I began to burn sage and became drawn to all things Native American. On another occasion, another guide came in, and I studied acupuncture and eastern medicine.

Soon I realized I could ask for all areas of learning, and I began nagging for assistance with my painting and writing pursuits. To advantage the outcome I asked for these specific teachers to come in a few days or weeks before I painted or wrote. This gave the guide and I, time to acclimatize to each other.

We can ask for teachers to assist us with any creative or learning pursuit. There are plenty of guides willing to work with us. All we need to do is ask and let them in. If you know someone who is struggling to write a book or studying a particular subject you can ask on their behalf. Sometimes you can struggle to complete something or lose your way so extra spiritual experts can help enormously. Over the years, I have requested that family and others be sent support when studying for exams, writing books, painting and completing their pursuits. Be assured the right helpers will arrive, and the person's soul can access them. As with all of this work, I send it with love and with the person's right to accept or not.

Spiritual teachers can happily guide you to people who are on earth, who can teach you, refer you to the books you need or guide you to the appropriate courses to attend.

Once we become connected to our teachers wonderful experiences follow. Often I would wake up in the morning and "know" a new idea or skill. By "know" I mean to understand how something works and to be able to do something different to the way I did it before. As we become used to the means we can work with Spirit here on earth the connection will strengthen.

Over time our energy and theirs will meld and the exchange of information becomes easier. My paintings are constantly changing. They are less challenging to create, as my painting guardians and I are becoming as one.

There is so much we can access from the universe. Our intention to ask for the information will enable us to learn all we need. Our wish to call in teachers to help will further our progress. Ask and you will receive.

Learning in spiritual healing rooms

When I began to do the work, I wanted to know everything. I would ask to be taught in the spiritual healing rooms. During these times, I would wake up and remember working on certain individuals. Occasionally, those same people would turn up on my doorstep weeks or months later. There were times when halfway through a healing, I would remember already having worked on them. It was like the angels gave me a practice run first.

If you want to increase your skills in the healing areas go to the rooms at night. Here you are instructed while you sleep. The healing rooms look like crystal palaces to me with pearly, crystal tables to work on and beautiful lights shining through the windows. I recollect many different healers working there with me. Exquisite music filled the air as I listened and practiced. The next morning when I woke up, I would just know how to do things. It was exciting.

The universe is full of information, so tap into it. The internet is similar to the universe in a way. We only have to know where to go, and how to access the information. It is all there waiting for us to find.

Going to the healing rooms

When asleep you can visit and be visited by Spirit. It is a good idea to ask to be taken to the healing rooms. There you can have healing done on yourself at a very high level. Everyone has times we need more help. At these times ask to revisit the healing rooms. Not only can healing be done, but our vibrational rate can be raised.

After the night has passed you may feel no different, but be patient. Remember, this type of work can take days, weeks, months or years to be manifest in your physical world. Of course, there are times when you can feel the difference immediately. Other times, you may receive messages and have insights you weren't aware of before. While you lie there on the crystal table with the light shining through the crystal glass, they work on you and talk to you about things you need to know. On the nights when I visit the healing rooms I invariably sleep very heavily. I don't remember anything. However, over the next few days the insights come, and I feel that the healing I asked for has been given.

The angels are always willing to heal, help and guide you; we only have to ask. At first I felt unsure about whether the healing was really occurring. Then a very psychic friend of mine in Finland told me she saw a picture of me. In her vision, I was lying on a table surrounded by angels working on me. It was the validation I needed. I was blown away.

We can also ask for others to go with us to the healing rooms. I have taken many people to the rooms with me. There we lie on tables near each other receiving the work. Keep in mind that no one will come with us, unless on a soul level they want to. It will always be their choice.

Many people would not be able even to consider doing this on a human level, but as souls they will make a different choice.

I have met very enlightened people who block healing on a soul level. Although their human side says they want to heal, they can't receive it. On the other hand, I have met the skeptic who can receive on a soul level. Never assume who will come with you on this journey, for this is soul work and only the soul knows.

The healing rooms are a powerful way to advance your healing and spiritual awareness, so ask to go whenever you feel the need to connect.

Visiting the learning libraries

At the beginning of my spiritual journey, I read anything I could get my hands on about these matters, and I practiced my healing and channeling skills whenever and wherever I could.

In time, I realized I could receive more information by visiting the learning libraries in the "sky." Every night I would ask to visit these rooms. Initially, I would visualize myself walking up the stairs, climbing up to the front door and walking into the area I wished to learn from. While I was interested in herbs, I went to that section. When I was going through my essential oil stage, I would go to that part of the library. Once in that section I would read the particular books held there in the halls of wisdom.

After a few weeks, I would find a curious thing happening. I would just know what herb to use. I realized I had not learnt it here because I actually knew nothing about the particular plant. After a session in which I told the client to use a certain herb, I would research the herb and find out it was perfect for their condition. It was so confirming for me.

Since then I ask to visit the rooms for new information. Try it yourself. You can learn many interesting things while you are sleeping or in deep meditative states.

Asking for better outcomes for others

Everyone has their individual paths to walk. Some are easy. Some are very hard. There are those who have made poor choices, so the path ahead is steep and rocky. It can be difficult to watch others walk these dreadful paths. Initially, I tried to help these people as much as possible. However, in time, I realized I was not really helping at all.

We have all set up tricky situations to work through, for it is part of our growth. Over time, I understood that on many occasions, my attempts to help others proved to have negative effects. I began to realize when my actions were of help and when they were simply interference. We are here to assist others, not do their lessons. If we step in and attempt to do their lessons, their learning is compromised.

In general, intervention can slow the person's progress. By carrying them, they can't learn the lesson by themselves. The lesson will continue to present until they have done it on their own. So think carefully before you offer to sort out other people's problems. Be aware that in your effort to assist, you could unwittingly be interfering with their progress.

Help on this level is powerful and non-controlling. With this request to Spirit it became easier to accept the outcomes, and I could willingly step back allowing the lesson to run its course. In asking for a less painful journey for the person I knew that Spirit would help.

I have witnessed the work of Spirit with people that I have asked help for. At times, the outcomes came to a head surprisingly soon, and new paths were shown or the pain the person needed to endure was lessened, a bit like being given a local anesthetic.

All is possible in our world, so never forget it.

Healing through Dreams

*Look back to learn. For we only
need the enlightenment to shine the road ahead.*

Dreams as spiritual signs

Dreams can be a powerful medium to gain more insights. I am not talking about dreams that may be connected to what you watched on television last night. I refer to the dreams you remember that deal with issues in your life. Personally, I think deciphering dreams can be difficult. There are countless books explaining what everything means with stock explanations of each scenario. Honestly, I find this a simplistic view of dreams because dreams serve several purposes.

Dreams fit into two basic categories. There are our soul dreams and there are our human dreams. Deciding, which one is which, takes practice.

In my understanding, human dreams reflect human experiences. They come from our daily lives and contain recognizable features. Without fail, they are a jumble of bizarre events and people. It is here we are dating a gorgeous film star or maybe being chased by terrorists. Some parts of recent films we have watched or events cross over into our world and generally, there are no messages or insights, only a series of random events. Human dreams are by nature eclectic.

Soul dreams are very different. Our soul is always trying to speak to us. In these dreams information can come through easily without human interference. Soul dreams can have a strong emotional component. I have noticed that when I am woken up by a dream that I can recall it vividly. When I remember it later in the day it is with absolute clarity, as though the dream has just happened.

Before I was ready to face my childhood trauma, I had a lot of soul dreams. Well, they were more like nightmares. These dreams were so intense they would leave me reeling for days.

Obviously, while my human side was blocking, my soul was trying to bring my past to the surface through the dreams.

Some dreams are so obscure that you can't understand the storyline or work out the bizarre happenings. In my quest to understand my dreams, I recognized that the story was not as important as the feelings I was experiencing. The question I asked myself was "What is the predominant feeling in the dream?"

Soul dreams are about emotions at the deepest level. The most common feelings are fear, anger, loss and frustration. Acknowledging these feelings enables us to explore and tackle our issues. In our human world, we have to hide deep emotions, whereas dreams allow acknowledgement and expression of these emotions.

I know we dream to heal, for it is in the expression of emotions that we gain further understanding of ourselves. Then we can begin to deal with our problems. It is healing for us to allow the expression through the dream-state instead of bottling up our emotions. Our soul is free to feel and talk. Angry dreams allow us to scream, swear and beat up characters real or imaginary. Dreams are our own video games. We get to act out our feelings and hurt no one in the process. In acting out in our dreams, we can connect to our deepest emotions and recognize their existence. The process is cathartic for us.

When I scream and attack someone in a dream, I am able to release great anger. I heal my unexpressed rage on a soul platform. Then, by remembering it, I face my emotions in the human world.

Occasionally, we can have a run of release dreams. Perhaps you have decided you want to let go of some fear from your aura. Don't be surprised if in the coming weeks and months

Spiritual Answers to Guide Your Life

your nights are filled with running, chasing and scary dreams. You are releasing the fear on a deep level.

Dreams can be keys to acknowledging what is going on in relationships. I have had dreams with people not wanting to be with me and months later the friendships changed. These signs are your soul talking directly to your human by using these warning dreams. When you have disturbing dreams, don't take them literally. If you dream your son dies in an accident, don't jump to conclusions. Ask yourself, "What was the basic feeling I had in the dream?" Normally, it will be fear, your fear of loss. Maybe recently someone else has died, and it has touched off your own fears regarding death. We all fear loss. A death or dying dream can undoubtedly signify a change. Keep in mind, not all dreams are psychic messages. On the whole, they are our deepest emotions being expressed.

Countless people are scared of their dreams. Some hate going to sleep due to recurrent and terrible nightmares. These terrors are found within us. I think these dreams are simply to awaken our human awareness and get us to deal with our own monsters so to speak.

Dreams are a way to clear old emotional blocks, so I suggest you look at what your fears are if you are experiencing many nightmares. Through developing self-awareness, you will be in a better position to address your fears, frustrations and anger. Maybe in the process you can find outlets for these emotions.

Psychic dreams are different to ordinary dreams. Usually I have known that the dream contained a psychic message. In my heart, there was no doubt. Psychic dreams talk to you. They don't come from your human feelings. They can also have an observer quality to them, as though we are in the dream and at the same time watching it play out. One salient point is highlighted in these dreams as you are guided to the outcome. The rest of the dream pales into the background, and you remember the one significant message.

Over time, you will find it easier to understand your dreams. Dreams are often sorting out the jumbles of the day, while some guide you to understand your current situation. I believe being able to decipher the most important messages from your dreams will bring peace and clarity into your life.

Traveling to other places in dreams

In my opinion, traveling in dreams is basically astral traveling. As a child, I remember experiencing dreams in which I could fly. However, they were not strictly dreams. Whilst asleep, I traveled outside my physical body via what is known as the astral or soul body, crossing both time and space. All is possible in the world of Spirit.

I enjoy flying dreams. For the most part, they are my escape from this dense body. The human body is very heavy, and while asleep it is possible to escape from the constraints of the human world.

I know that we can meet other people and spiritual beings, once sleep comes. There are many people who undertake to do spiritual work at night when they temporarily leave their bodies. Healers can visit other people all over this world or worlds beyond and give healing using their spiritual body. They are able to transcend time and space. How amazing is that?

Meeting those from the other side

Everyone knows we can meet others in the dream-state. Lots of us have reunited with deceased relatives and friends at night. These dreams are vivid and it feels like they really happened. That is because it did, in fact, happen, it just occurred in another dimension. On a level, we know we dreamt it; however, we know that on a soul level, it literally happened. Of course, to attend these meetings we needed to leave our physical bodies, for out of our human form, we are able to transgress time and space.

These times allow us to find a way to meet deceased ones again and be together once more. I find it a wondrous event. Generally, I can't really remember all the conversations, and mostly recall more about how it felt when we were reunited.

There are many reasons for these sojourns. The paramount one is to reconnect for mutual benefit. Being able to be together again is a gift. Once death has occurred it can be difficult to reach one another. The dream-state makes it easier.

If in the past, some issues have not been resolved with a person, then through reuniting new understandings can be reached. Not everyone has the opportunity for closure. Some people are not physically close when the other person's death occurred. Sometimes the circumstances surrounding the passing don't lend themselves to communication. In the dream-state much can be sorted out in a place of love and peace.

Some people meet in dreams because they need the connection with the person. Maybe it is the only way. Not everyone can visit a medium or be open to the spiritual side of life. This avenue offers a safe and private way to communicate.

There are special times when the deceased ones come into the dream-state to warn you. Perhaps your car brakes need replacing or someone needs to be alerted to a situation. In the dream, they will tell you, and you will remember when you awaken. Warnings from Spirit come in many guises. Dreams are a common medium.

It is very common for people to return to apologize in the dream-state. It benefits both parties. It is an apology on a soul level and as such becomes a healing for those involved. After souls have been in the healing rooms, they can see the damage they have done. We are frequently unaware of our actions on earth. However, once we cross over all is revealed, we can view our lives and see the damage we may have incurred.

I love the dream meetings because it is so lovely to be able to spend time with the departed person. One of my friends who died recently visited me, and she looked radiant. We were unable to see one another before her death and never had a chance to be together again in the earthly realm. For me, it was a wonderful closure to a special friendship, and I was honored that she chose to visit me.

I cherish any dreams where these souls return to us.

Sorting out relationships in dreams

This section is unlike the previous one in that all the parties in the dream meetings continue to live here on earth. Maybe they live close to us, maybe not. In this dream-state, we meet on a soul level first to discuss issues we may be having in this life.

In my life, I have had many of these dreams. I would wake knowing I was with a family member or friend talking through the current problems. Frequently, I have recalled most of the finer details. There are times when we can't reach people. One reason can be distancing. Another is if we are estranged from the person and communication may be non-existent.

Sometimes a topic can't be discussed on the human level yet. Perhaps we are not quite ready to go there. Here the dream-state is a safe medium. The discussions we have in the dream-state can be resolved. I have remembered having in-depth talks with the person in my dreams. Then several weeks later the same conversation occurs in real time. The conversation in our dream had filtered down into our human world.

Besides the above, dreams are expressions, a place to vent without hurting anyone. The conversations or even arguments we have in this state can allow us to release unhealthy emotions. They can alert us to the depth of our anger or grief. With this new understanding, we then have an opportunity to process and work on these hidden aspects of ourselves.

Regularly meeting on a spiritual level through dreams has healing power. It gives our souls the opportunity to open doors to growth and understanding. There is the potential for great healing via dreams.

Meeting your guides

We have already met our guides when we sleep, yet few of us realize this fact. When this occurs, we can be free from all worldly concerns and be with our guardians. In this space, no one is pressing us to do something, and there are no distractions. During these times, we can all discuss the necessary issues and plan ahead. I think much future planning is done in the dream-state.

Lots of spiritually minded individuals want to meet their personal guides. It is easy to do. Initially, ask to meet in dreams and ask them for signs of the nightly meetings. As your connection with your guides strengthens you will recognize that these meetings are occurring. I have found with practice you can train yourself to bring these memories to the front of your mind. However, like all spiritual practices it takes time and commitment.

Gradually, over time, you may visualize how your guides look, and you may get an idea of their personality or a name runs through your head. It does not matter how the information comes to you. It will be in a way you can decipher.

Remember, we are in constant contact with our helpers every day and every night.

The Creative Power of our Minds

The mind does not differentiate between reality and thought, for both are seen as the same. So think what you wish to do or where you wish to be and the mind will respond.

The mind/body orbs

The mind and the body are like two overlapping circles. They are independent of one another, and yet dependent on each other. This equal and linked relationship ensures balance in the aura. While both orbs are working in this way, we maintain health. However, once the balance changes, it will be reflected in the aura, and the energy flow will be compromised.

The mind is regularly given more importance than the body. Even so, although it is powerful, we are nothing on the earth plane without the body. Both have equal importance to our well-being. I don't see it as mind/body connection. Rather, it is the mind and the body working together. When the two orbs shift, it is reflected in the aura. For example, if the mind changes the body is directly affected, for, even though each orb can function autonomously of one another, they are linked.

Some people only live through their mind. They do not acknowledge their body. We meet these people everywhere. They are the ones who come into work coughing with the flu, taking no notice that their body needs them to go home and rest. They are found running marathons with bleeding feet or exercising until they physically throw up. Disconnection like this is common and typically seen in a positive light by society. The negative side to this way of living is that eventually the body will over-ride the mind and simply break down.

The mind can ignore the body for only so long. The body will work until its survival is threatened, then it takes over. If you need to work through something and are living only in your mind, your mind keeps an eye on how your body is responding. Learn to do, likewise. Listen to your body. Allow it to rest, eat, drink and recuperate when it needs to. The mind is an important part of you, but it is not more important than the body.

They both need each other here on earth.

Once we view the mind/body orbs overlapping, it will be easier to understand the need for autonomy and cooperation. The balance is important. There will be times when one orb will over-ride the other. These times can regularly be accommodated by either the mind or the body. However, if the imbalance lasts too long the depleted orb will eventually revert to prioritize itself. If it is the mind it will over-ride the body and vice versa.

When I finally understood the fine balance between the mind and body I changed how I lived. I had been traumatized as a child. I had learnt how to live in my mind hardly acknowledging my body as a unit unto itself. My mind won every time. I would soldier on using the power of my mind.

Eventually, my body took over. It was only then I began to listen to my body's voice. It was not by choice, but through necessity. Over time, I have worked to improve the balance. These days I respect the needs of the body and do not see it as less than the mind.

When we come to an understanding of how mind and body work together every aspect of our life will become better. The body screams out when it is not heard. It hurts and pains, and if we do not pay attention or take appropriate action, we will suffer the consequences of poor health. Therefore, take note of the warning signs. You feel with your body. It talks to you all the time. You just need to learn to listen and follow its guide. Once you make contact with your body's inner dialogue you can give it what it needs.

Your mind signals by thought. It speaks to you via your thinking patterns. Your mind is extremely important, as your thoughts help to propel you into action. Follow your mind's direction. Much information comes from the mind, which directly influences your body. If your thoughts are based on love and peace you will feel calm within your body. Conversely, negative thinking and fearful or angry thoughts will disturb the delicate balance of the body.

Try to give both orbs equal time and energy. Aim to balance the body and mind. Remember, the mind communicates with thought, and the body communicates with feelings.

Once you learn this basic truth about the orbs your whole life will take on a new light. I believe that by spending time and effort meeting the needs of your mind and body, your life will be balanced and at peace.

The thinking brain and the soul mind

Our human brain is in our physical body. It operates the human part of us existing in the third dimension. It is very important to understand that we are more than just the human body. We are a soul living in a physical body. For clarity in this chapter I will refer to the human mind as our thinking brain. The human mind is in our brain. We also have a soul mind which lives in all dimensions, and is not confined to the body. The soul mind can move out of our human form.

I believe the soul mind runs our thinking brain, using it to operate in our human world. Even though the thinking brain performs many tasks to keep everything functioning, it does not really control our lives as many people like to think.

Your soul mind is in control of you. It can move into other dimensions and is not confined to earth. Your soul mind resonates in every part of you, and it has a cell consciousness down to the smallest manifestation. On this atomic level is reflected everything your soul mind contains.

The human brain has limitations. The soul mind has none. The soul mind thinks differently to the human one. The thinking brain operates in human patterns of thought and structure, whereas the soul mind is without boundaries.

We all possess the soul mind. It sits in the soul body and travels with us through time and space. Unlike the thinking brain, it has less prejudice, and it has more freedom. The soul mind does not die. People affected by mental illness or in a coma continue to have an active soul mind. Death or injury can destroy the thinking brain, but the soul mind lives on forever.

When we try to talk to someone's higher self, we are connecting to their soul mind. I know the thinking brain cannot communicate in this way, because being three-dimensional it cannot be accessed telepathically.

Your soul mind belongs to you, and it contains all the information you have gleaned in your lives. It is expansive, allowing you to access information from all dimensions. You can use your soul mind to remember all that has been. In fact, it is part of the universal mind, so the idea of us needing to connect to the universal mind is a man-made structure.

The thinking brain has inherent blocks and is unable to comprehend the workings of the universe. The human view is narrow and incomplete, whilst the soul mind view is expansive and panoramic. We may not have the words or explanations for the information coming in. We just know it is.

Spiritual work with the soul mind

When we do spiritual work, we use the soul mind, not the human one. The thinking brain can convert some concepts, but it cannot access the spiritual work. It has a three-dimensional or, in some people who have advanced in this life, a four-dimensional quality. In my opinion, we could call the soul mind the engine and the thinking brain the cogs.

Once mankind acknowledges this basic truth, we will make great strides forward. In a sense, our brain mentality holds us back. I remember having a discussion with a medical student about the existence of the brain and mind. She maintained the brain was the mind, but I argued the soul mind sits in the brain and extends out from it. The soul mind is not contained in the brain, but can travel to other dimensions using its own energy.

At this time, we have not discovered a convincing way to measure soul mind energy with a machine. That time will come, and it will be mind-blowing for some! I can't wait! It will be the merging of the spiritual and scientific worlds.

You can use the soul mind to perform most energy work and bring about change. All we need is the intention. Focus on an issue, send love and healing, and it will be done. We all carry the Light. Some of us are aware of our ability, while others are not.

You only have to have the intention to send light for it to occur. You don't have to meditate for weeks or join a group and pay large amounts of money to learn, for all the skills are at your fingertips. We are all beings of light, and we can send light with a thought.

The soul mind is the medium for relaying energetic information. For instance, prayers and healing are conveyed via soul mind. When hundreds of people send love and healing using their soul mind, all the soul minds connect. I have seen the individual soul lights. They join up forming a net of light all around the earth. It is a beautiful and wondrous sight. If we all sent light, good thoughts and healing our soul minds would expand and be able to make many energetic shifts in our world.

Spirit connects via the soul mind. Energetically, it is the best avenue for communication. You can ask for clarification or knowledge on a soul mind level, but keep in mind that it takes time to filter down into your conscious brain.

When you focus with your soul mind you can use it to collect lots of information. It has been my experience that I would simply wake up and know things. I did not read it or experience it. I just knew the information to be true. There were times I could not understand all the parts of it. I just accepted what my soul mind was telling me.

We are beginning to explore the untapped power of the soul mind. The best is yet to come!

The universal mind

The universal mind is everything. Each one of us is part of the universal mind. Our soul minds are part of the greater universal mind, and we all exist in this sea of energy, and can access this mind. It is not separate from each of us, for we are all a small microcosm of the larger form.

Once you realize your mind is sharing in the universal mind your whole life can change. In recognizing this incredible truth, your vision can expand. Energetically, it opens up another world for you. You can be free to gather more information and understand the way our universe works. You

Spiritual Answers to Guide Your Life

are no longer limited by your own human perception, for you are greater than you imagine. You are the universe, and the universe is you.

The universal mind is like a swirling mass of energy and can be reached by thought. So if I want to know something I communicate directly with the universal mind. We all know how to access this information on a soul level. Unfortunately, once we reach the denseness of the earth we forget how to do it.

The universal mind is where all the bright ideas and new inventions originate from, and many people have been able to download the information and manifest it on earth. How many times do we hear of someone getting an idea that just "popped" into their head? People "download" songs and works of art using the same process.

An intriguing phenomenon happens with the universal mind. As a rule, an idea, song or invention is floating around within the universal mind. So somewhere in the world, intentionally or not, several soul minds can download it. Many times numerous minds have accessed it at the same time. Within days, on the earth plane, the same idea is manifesting in several parts of the world. All those people are unconsciously tapping into the universal mind.

Ideas in the universal mind are energy. They can be converted and made to manifest in our human world. Despite our belief that it is all our idea I have come to realize that we tap into the universal mind in this way, and this is really how man has developed through all time.

I see our soul mind is the universal mind, as they are one inside the other.

Tapping into the universal mind requires commitment and patience. You need to be aware of where you are in your development. For example, if you want to know a difficult scientific solution, you will need some understanding of science to access the answer. The greater your own knowledge, the further you can go with your "download." Be aware that the process can be supported by people in your field, by books and exposure to your chosen field. You might need to meet similar professionals with whom to learn and work with. Remember, we are in a physical dimension so physical areas have to be set up for our learning.

Timing comes into play. Maybe you are not in the right place yet for the answers to be given regarding your area. You may have set up other learning to do at this time. Then the download will have to wait. The people you were supposed to work with may be unavailable. The books you have to read might not be published yet. Just because the answer does not come immediately does not mean it won't. All good things come to those who wait.

There is always help at hand. Spirit is always trying to support our endeavors. They hear our cries for the answers and try to provide them. If we ask for knowledge from the universal mind, it will come. Be patient and all will unfold.

Minds from other dimensions

Not all people come here with the same experiences. I believe there are many who come from very different dimensions. Earth is only a construct, a play in which we can learn many lessons. Although many think we are all there is, this world is far behind other dimensions, especially in the areas of understanding how to use energy. At this time others from more advanced dimensions are here to facilitate our advancement in these areas.

These souls will look like everyday people, but that is where it ends. Their soul will be very different. Soul groups are on earth from other galaxies bringing with them their light and knowledge to assist in our human world. The reason they chose to come to help was due to their understanding of other dimensions. They are on a mission, as their work is to advance the world.

If you are reading this book you could be one of them.

I recognize these souls by their utter bewilderment of how it works on our earth. Notably, these souls can't settle and question everything. Frequently, they wonder if this is all there is. Although on a soul level, they know the reason, their human remains confused. You may have felt the same or met people displaying these responses.

I suspect these souls work predominately through the soul mind and only use the human mind to function and fit into this world. Their ability to access universal knowledge is easy for them because the channel is open and without bounds. Consequently, they will think differently to someone working mostly with the human mind. I don't think they are better than a human. However, their access to information is more universal.

Others originate from dimensions, we can't even fathom. From these strange worlds comes much new information that can be useful to our earth. Knowledge is endless. It has no beginning or end, just an energetic loop expanding and changing, like the Light.

Perhaps reading this section resonates with you. Maybe you are one of these souls struggling with life on earth. The easiest way to cope is to embrace your difference. Know you are not like others and accept you may have lived in other dimensions. There can be a kind of peace once we embrace our uniqueness.

I believe knowing about yourself can open up huge possibilities; a world without limits.

Akashic records

All through time we have been aware of a library in the sky. In this library, we all have our personal books of life containing all of our sojourns through time and space. This vast place holds all we have done. It contains our own personal book of life. It also records universe information. Seers through the ages have used this library to tap in and access information. The Akashic records are where we go to get information when we channel. From the records, we can relay important past lives and personal details for the person having the reading. Within the library is held the history of our world and other dimensions. There is a wealth of knowledge, if we know how to access it.

The best way is via the soul mind, not the thinking brain. This mind can span out of our three-dimensional life and into other planes if we allow it. Being connected to the universal mind we can travel and explore these expansive books of life. Developing this gift allows us to be free from a limited way of viewing life. In a funny way, we have to use the human mind to free the soul mind. The greater freedom we allow ourselves, the greater the access.

Tapping into the Akashic records makes an energetic connection, so the information can be downloaded and converted in our own brain. However, remember that some concepts held in the records are almost incomprehensible to our thinking brain. So we have to find a way to make sense of it, as it can get lost in translation.

Whenever I am allowed to read another person's book I do so with regard to their own sacred space and personal rights. In reality, it is really Spirit who accesses the information and speaks to them. I am only the channel, no more, no less. With a pure intention, you can help others to gain access to their own Akashic records. It is wonderful to relay past lives and gifts to others and, in knowing more they begin to see their own vastness.

By visiting the records, we can gain tremendous understandings about previous journeys and lessons. In this life, we can choose to activate unacknowledged gifts and skills. I think it is so fabulous. I have asked to visit my own book and be given access to my lives, so I can call on all the positive parts of those spiritual lives. I have requested that gifts and knowledge be made known to me, so I can advance personally and spiritually. To strengthen your access use meditation and when in that sacred space, the records can be easily gained.

When your guardians think the time is right you might find you can start to read your own book. How interesting and exciting would that be?

Telepathy

Our soul never needs to speak as our highest form of communication is telepathic. Although we have invented speech and languages for our time on earth, we speak best when we speak with our soul minds only. This is a true energetic connection.

When I had my accident and crossed over to the other side my mother was waiting. She was standing about ten meters from me on the other side of a river. Although she communicated with me, her mouth never moved. Both of us were using mental telepathy, only speaking with our minds. It was when I returned to earth again that I realized she had not spoken to me. I had only heard her thoughts.

There is a big difference between human talking and soul speech. As humans we are taught what to say and when to say it. We are taught to read the situation and only say what will be accepted, and for most of the time we learn to talk in a way that society dictates. We lie and say things even we don't believe. We leave things unsaid, and manipulate others with our words. Think one thing, yet say another. Human communication is stilted and guarded, coming from the head, not from the soul. Often while all this is happening our soul is still and simply observes.

If only we could see the power of our innate gift; with telepathy, the world could advance dramatically. Every thought has power energetically. We don't have to be with the other person to communicate because our thoughts travel directly to the person we are thinking about. When people think about us a connection is made. We are all connected energetically, telepathically linked. Our thoughts are energy and as such have the power to alter another person's energy field in a dramatic way. Thinking of them and having positive thoughts will affect their aura. The contrary is also true. If we are angry or upset with someone they will pick it up telepathically.

People normally connect energetically first. Many are intellectually unaware of this fact, even though we "know" it happens frequently. So much happens on an energetic level that most of us are not really aware of it in our daily lives. In truth, this telepathic connection is where our soul truly speaks. I am sure it is here, in this place, that much healing can take place. Our telepathic thoughts are more than words; they carry with them all of our emotions as well.

Once you understand the power of telepathy you can work at improving this gift. By focusing on those around, you can improve your energetic response to them and in so doing strengthen your own skills. Everyone is telepathic, even if they scoff at the idea. All of us have had the experience where we have thought of someone and shortly thereafter we receive a call, or we have been wondering how a person is and then bump into them at the shops.

In my experience, those from the other side can talk to us telepathically. You may find yourself thinking a lot about your deceased mum or friend. At those times, I know our souls are talking to each other. This is a sign of telepathy crossing time and space.

I am sure there are people with whom we share telepathic connections, even when apart. This can have both positive and negative outcomes. While these relationships may be over, the telepathic links can continue. We can tune into each other even when no contact exists in the human world. Sometimes we can't be together. Circumstances change and the physical relationship is no more. Yet, our telepathic connection can be as strong or even stronger, to the degree that we can sense how they are, or if they are ill or unhappy.

Telepathic links are energetic "hook-ins". When we are day-dreaming about someone we are linking up energetically. I always know when someone is thinking of me. As a rule, I know it is them making the link because I have not been thinking of them. Then into my head they enter and maybe stay for a few days. You might be able to recall similar circumstances.

The reverse can occur. You can call them into your field by thinking about them. On some level, they will pick up your connection. When I think in this way I try to send good thoughts and love, but not everyone does.

There are people who use their telepathic ability to control or upset others. This is a very bad karmic practice! Perhaps one partner has decided to move on and begin a new life. Still hurting from the disappointment of the break-up, they are fragile and vulnerable. There are those who can pick up on this telepathically and prey on it. How many times have we witnessed one person trying to move on, when the ex turns up to disrupt everything again? The ex is picking up energetically that the other person is moving forward and tries to sabotage their progress. These souls are using telepathy. Once they sense the other person is moving away from their grasp, they will try to pull them back. In returning to the relationship, nothing really changes and frequently all the ex does is to cause even more pain and confusion.

People telepathically sense illness or impending disaster. These messages come in strongly and without any tangible base. Most people can't help but connect physically to settle their constant worry. In many cases, the telepathic link proves to be right. In tribal cultures, telepathy is respected and followed without question. When we lived in Africa it was common place. Our house-boy announced one day that he had to go home as he knew his father was ill. No one stopped him. Arriving home his telepathic message proved to be correct. Maybe without our modern, sophisticated communication system back then, we learnt to tune into our instincts and follow them.

A similar telepathic incident happened in our family. My husband's mother left the office to go home because she knew something was wrong. When she arrived home her father had just died. The exact time she picked it up telepathically at work was when he had died at home.

Once we begin to tune in, it is amazing how we all link up. There is a whole complex telepathic system operating throughout our society. As we advance vibrationally, our ability to tune in will dramatically improve. In the future we can become like the telepathic people from Atlantis.

Calling in telepathically

We are all energy. Each of us is energetically unique, but essentially we are similar walking, talking auras. As such, we are able to connect to one another on this energetic level. Knowing this universal truth allows us to "call" someone from the past or future into our lives.

At one stage in my life, I wanted to meet more women like me. My friendships had changed and I was craving women interested in the aspects of life I was now learning about. Spirit helped me connect with them in a very simple manner. I was guided to visualize these women as energy fields out there somewhere. Next, I was directed to call them in, with the understanding that only those who wanted to answer the call would come. Free will is paramount in these types of connections.

It is the soul calling the soul. This kind of energetic intention can bring a relationship forward in time as it operates on another level to a human request.

Not only can it bring in new relationships. It can speed up relationships that are already on their way. Once the call is made, everything can quicken. Perhaps you were meant to meet in six months time and now with the energetic connection it may be shortened to one or two months.

Single people can call in a new partner using the same technique. In my experience, I have found some single people are so because on some deep level they feel safer being single. This feeling comes from a fear of being hurt again or not trusting in their ability to make a good choice of partner. These emotions form blocks around their aura and can sabotage any opportunity to be in a romantic relationship. We all send out energetic signals to others, and I think their signal is telling the potential partners to "keep away from me." I have one girl whose signal is so strong that Ray and I can feel the "prickles" emanating from her aura. If you are single and want to be in a relationship maybe you can relate to this, or if you have a single friend you can now understand where they are coming from. In my opinion, being able to understand the dynamics at work can help to release these old blocks and open us up to new worlds.

If you choose to "call" in a new romantic partner use the same method as I have described above. Be clear in your mind concerning the type of person you wish to meet. A useful guide is to ask the spiritual world for the best partner for you to be manifest in your world.

We all have our own energetic signal, and others can find us by this invisible signal. Sending out the welcoming signal will reach the other person. Our positive intention makes for a stronger attraction. In other words, we are easier to find when we consciously put out the welcome mat.

Timing is crucial on the earthly plane, therefore, be aware that divine timing can influence your call to Spirit. Free will and choice can speed up or block things.

In my work, I have noticed it is not only single people who are scared to be in some friendships. We can express wanting to be attached, while we continue to put up blocks around our aura. Like those single people, these blocks are a form of protection from being hurt again. It can be hard to trust yourself and others when you have been deeply hurt. Be aware of your blocks and try to release them when you want to call in new relationships.

Over the years, I have "called in" for other people too. Maybe your friend needs a new partner or some more friends. Once you understand the process you can directly call in the energy of others for them. All spiritual work like this will come from the loving heart. Spirit can bring new opportunities for your friend. They will then have the choice to accept or not. Many people need help to find their way. This is a simple, but effective way to assist in their journey.

Once I knew how to use this method I could work on providing all I needed. Some of us who have moved so much spiritually may find our friendships have also moved and changed dramatically. Although we understand on a soul level, it can be quite hard on a human level. Knowing I could signal to others more like me gave me hope of new and wonderful friendships filling my world again.

Higher self

Everyone has a higher self. The higher self is the soul at its best. In my opinion, it is where we go for direction, and it is where our own truth really exists. There can be times when in our human world, we can't talk to someone. Essentially we can't truly speak our mind here. Social etiquette and life in general can make open communication almost impossible. Maybe we are estranged or the person won't be able to deal with the subject or idea we wish to put forward.

In these scenarios, I suggest you go directly to their higher self and talk to them. When I say talk, I mean to focus on them and say what you need to say to them. The way I do this is I find a quiet moment and think of the person. Then I begin a dialogue, just as if they are right with me and tell them what I feel, what I truly think.

Everyone can be reached in this way. Whether they receive or listen becomes their choice.

I have found very resistant beings may try to block the information coming in. Timing is the key. If you were trying to send a message telepathically in December, but the person was not "receiving," that same message may not be activated until June. It will sit in suspension waiting for the right time. It is never lost. Like the healing, the soul will use it when the time is right. In that way others always have charge of their own personal power.

In speaking to the higher self we are trying to connect and reach an understanding. It is never about control, but opportunity. People can surprise you. In my experience, I have seen massive turnarounds in relationships where higher telepathy was used. When you work with telepathy on this level it enables you to work through the soul layers until it reaches the human dimension. It filters down until the work done can be manifest in our human world. This will be in the right time and space for each soul.

You can have frequent dialogue with the higher self. Once you learn how to tune in it becomes more and more like a human connection. These days when I am speaking to the higher selves of others, I can pick up their body language and their responses when I "talk" to them. At times, with some people you can feel the words coming back at you. It is as if the words bounce off them back to you. Don't give up when this happens. Persevere and in time the connection could improve. Anger and fear are common reasons for the "bounce."

Higher self talk results in the words filtering down and touching our human side and from this healing can occur. Always speak with love, even if you are still upset, because the love between you is more important. If, for some reason, there is little love, focus on the truth. When there have been terrible outcomes, in particular situations, it is not always easy to begin with love. We have to release the hurt and anger before love and forgiveness can follow.

When I began to experiment with this method of communication, I believe I was coming from my human self more than from my higher self. As I became more skilled at this telepathic conversation I began to speak more and more from the higher self. Beware of a self sabotaging aspect of this work. It can be hard to talk to some people's higher selves. Your own stubbornness and resistance can get in the way. With difficult relationships, I start small with the little I can do. As I break down my own walls, the dialogue can extend.

Higher self talk is challenging and not without its obstacles. However, with perseverance big shifts can be made. It is not about winning or controlling it is about being able to make a connection, even when on a human level, it is not possible. We have drawn these relationships into our lives for mutual learning. When communicating telepathically with others, we must trust that our words reach their higher self. Even if we cannot detect a change, the words and feelings are always recorded in their aura. It is like sending a letter in the mail. The recipient always has the choice to read your letter, or not.

When I began to speak to others via the higher self it felt good. Although in the human world things were not quite right, I knew that on a spiritual level, everything possible was being done. It gave me a sense of peace and completion.

Changing old mental patterns

We all carry old, comfortable ways of thinking. These patterns have been with us for so long they can be hard to recognize. I believe tackling mental patterns takes patience and insight. Everyone has their own take on the world. It defines who we are. However, not all the beliefs we carry are our truth. Many of our core values come from years of being told to think in a particular way. Early life is mainly where we picked up these patterns. We also brought them in from past lives.

While we are full of outdated ideas it is hard to embrace change. It is as if our old thought patterns fill up too much of our aura and then there is no room for fresh ideas and concepts to enter that space. In addition, our aura contains its own mind as well as overlapping into the universal mind. Limiting ourselves to only our sphere does not allow us fully to explore the universal mind.

It is here in the universal mind that billions of concepts and vast knowledge resides. I wanted to be able to access this information and replace my entire mindset and in doing so replace my former way of thinking. Releasing outdated ways takes determination. However, I feel that with so much change occurring in the world I need to let go of old patterns. Altering ourselves in these ways opens up great possibilities. Intention is all we need, and to trust Spirit will help manifest these changes. As they say, "Ask and you shall receive." We are constantly connected to the spiritual world. There is always help available for development.

Remember though, asking does not necessarily mean you will receive immediately. Our part is to acknowledge it will be done in universal time. Many times, people get disheartened with the spiritual idea of time. For us, a short time may mean one week, while for Spirit, a short time may be measured in years.

The most important thing is our intention to move forward. When and how it occurs may be out of our hands. I have decided to let go of useless patterns. Some I am aware of, while others are still a mystery to me. Over time, they will surface and be shown to me, and I hope, with new eyes I can decide whether they hold a place in my current life. Some patterns are worth retaining. They contain part of our essence, our soul, while others are social patterns. Not all are now appropriate to our ever-changing world.

Once we embark on the change, our horizons can widen. I liken it to learning from television or being able to utilize the internet; the difference is enormous. In time, you will see the changes in the way you think. As your mind becomes more open and flexible, your aura will be capable of greater expansion.

Throwing out limiting thought patterns is the most liberating act one can do.

Tornado

Changing our way of thinking is challenging work. Honestly, we become blind to our own thoughts. We may have been thinking in these ways in this life and many lives before. It is not uncommon for it to be so ingrained that our habits become unrecognizable to us.

Fortunately, I was shown a valuable visualization to assist in the shift. All you need to do is to visualize a beam of light coming down into your crown chakra. This beam resembles a tornado. Imagine it coming down and as it enters the head area it swirls around collecting old thought patterns and sucks them up and out. When I did it, I swirled down to my neck and then swirled back up through the top of my head. The process was easy. You bring the light tornado in, collect debris and release it out of the crown. When I was first given this visual I concentrated carefully. Once I could perform it easily I could use it quickly to keep shifting out unnecessary thinking. In the next few days and weeks, I began to sense the shift in my thoughts.

In removing the old ways I was making way for new ideas and more flexible thought patterns. We all hang on to comfortable ways, but if we want to grow, certain thoughts have to go.

Once I mastered the tornado technique, I sent the energy tornado to others. Of course, it was sent for soul approval by them. In days, I noticed a shift in their usual stand. New ideas that had been negated were now being considered.

Growth is all about releasing, so if we can change our thinking by using the tornado method every aspect of our life can move forward. I found it to be a fabulous method. Every time it feels necessary, I use the light tornado. The energetic use of light helps to speed up any process of change in our thinking. We are what we think, it defines us, but old modes from this life and other past lives can hold us back.

Our intention to release old patterns is all that is needed. The light will do the rest.

Visualization – making it work energetically

There are lots of books about visualization. They tell you how to do it. You do it and hope it works. In my experience visualization does not always work. I now understand why. To make a change we have to work on an energetic level. Affirmations and imagining are not as powerful without the energetic shift. Lots of us have done affirmations diligently and have been disappointed with the results.

I am not trying to say these processes don't work. I am saying that they work best when the energetic shift occurs. This is because it is the energy shift that dictates any permanent change. I believe it is only with an energetic shift that deep change can occur.

For example, say we to want to change our body shape. Thinking ourselves different will not always be enough. If there are parts we want to change, we have to move the energy out of that area. We need to attach an energy shift to our visualization. I wanted a slimmer waist. It was mostly for comfort and health reasons. When I did the work, I "saw" the energy that had collected around my middle and moved it out of my aura. I did not only see a slimmer me. Instead I simply moved the energy and released it out of my aura. I kept seeing it moving out and being replaced with light. In a sense I replaced the whole tire around my waist with light.

When you move and replace the energy with light, the change can happen. Everything begins in the energy field, so that is where you have to start to get permanent results. The physical body replicates the energy body. Think of the jelly mould concept. Ultimately, the shape of the energy body dictates the shape of the physical body.

Visualization with energy can shift emotional problems. I had a block around being unable to cry. Tears had never come easy. Visualizing me crying was not enough. I needed the energetic shift to support the affirmation. To advantage the process, I saw the energetic tears running down my face. I saw fat balls of energy tears filling up until they had to release. I had to move the energy in my own aura. At the time I had a skilled healer working with me who was helping in moving the energy. The outcome was positive, and between the two of us, we managed to help me cry.

The intention becomes a reality when you move the energy. When you use visualization and move the energy together, it creates a synergy that assists the change.

I suspect those who have mastered only visualization are unknowingly shifting their own energy. Lots of people instinctively know how to move energy around and when they do visualization the energy shift is really occurring. They may be aware of the dualistic process or not.

Knowing why my visualization was not working was a revelation. When the energy you wish to move is layered, it may require many sessions. You cannot only do the visualization once and expect results, because some energy is hard to move. It could have been there for many lifetimes, therefore, be patient and know that with your visualization and the energy movement you are chipping away at it. In time the rewards will become clear.

All spiritual work needs your time and devotion. Never see your numerous attempts as signs of failure. Once you practice the technique you can work towards changing whatever you wish, for all is possible in the world of Spirit.

Feeling your visualization

There is another interesting aspect, apart from the energy movement, that can help your visualization work. As mentioned in the last chapter, we may have read all the books, been open to the secrets unveiled and done the work. I had done all the visuals too. In the money department, I had seen the dollars coming to us. Even so, the money situation remained the same. The other book was not published, and some personal wishes were not manifesting. My real world was not moving ahead.

It is discouraging to do so much work and seem to make little progress. Even with the energy shifting visual, I was missing something. Maybe you have felt like me. I had thought all the thoughts, written all the wishes and cut out the visuals and pasted them onto cardboard sheets. Then overnight I realized what the missing part was. I was using my mind. I was thinking it all and wishing. Nevertheless, I was not "feeling" the change. I was totally blown away when something so obvious was revealed to me.

We manifest all our dreams from the soul and the soul feels everything. I believe we draw to us what we feel, not what we think. I had to feel loved to attract love. I needed to feel financially secure to be so. I had to feel healthy to be well. It all seemed so clear. All those months I sent out my visuals, I did not feel rich. I felt poor. I felt I never had enough money. To change my financial world, I had to shift gears. I needed to "feel" wealthy and by projecting this emotional state, I could alter my universe.

We do attract what we feel, more so than we think. I had lots of single friends who expressed their wish for a good companion. Be that as it may, it wasn't happening. They wanted love, but felt unloved. They felt rejection, rather than acceptance. Their inherent feelings kept reflecting back into their lives. All their mantras and affirmations could not shift them. They had to make a shift in how they felt. By feeling loved, they could attract love. By feeling accepted and respected by others, they could draw it into their lives.

By addressing our feelings, we can change our lives, but we need to understand how we are feeling about a given situation. It is difficult to face our deepest emotions. I had come from a dysfunctional family. As a child I felt unlovable. I carried this emotion in my aura. During my life, I had frequently attracted those who supported my basic feelings. My life was being mirrored by others, and it was so powerful.

Initially, you may struggle to recognize your underlying emotions. You have been keeping those emotions hidden and so being honest with yourself can be challenging. Remember, like chewing gum these feelings will want to stick. They have been with us for so long.

Over time, I could recognize some of the negative emotions in me. In my quiet moment, I would become aware of them. It was like a light switched on, and I could finally see clearly. I did much soul-searching at these times. It is natural to stubbornly hold onto old emotional patterns. However, I asked that my stubbornness be released when I felt it was blocking me. I tried to observe my reactions in an effort to understand myself. I could see over time why I drew particular situations and relationships into my world repeatedly.

There can be many past-life emotions surfacing too. Issues with money and poverty were learnt in these times. Our emotions transfer into each life. Regardless of whether we can remember these past-life experiences just by recognizing our old lives will help with the shift.

Spiritual Answers to Guide Your Life

I found it helpful to ask those close to me to point out old emotional patterns. Others can be your eyes when we are blind. In the beginning, you might not like their input, and you may even argue the point, but try to see arguing as a signal. A signal you may be blocking the truth. If you can't handle what is being said at first you may find acceptance later. In a private moment, you can bring it out again and face it.

Remember, if we can't see an emotional problem, we can't change it.

Changing patterns brings many challenges. You might think it feels awkward when you initially alter an ingrained pattern. You may want to hang on to old ways because it will feel somehow comfortable and safe. It is usual to have these responses. However, to feel differently we have to let go of old habits. We have to find ways to feel loved, rich or accepted. It is all in how we interface with our world.

We have to learn how to feel our world differently. For example, when dealing with love, we need to feel love is all around. We need to recognize love is everywhere whether it is at home with our friends and family, at work with colleagues or on the bus when a child smiles at us.

To feel the new emotion you have to find it everywhere. Widen your focus and use all you have available. Draw from life's emotional well to heal. If you feel poor, you will draw a sense of poverty into your life. If you feel rich as you eat and partake in the world, you will attract abundance.

Once you begin to realize the importance of the emotions, you have discovered the key to change. I found it exciting and liberating to have been shown a new technique I could employ. Now, when things don't work out like I think they ought to, I ask these questions. "How do I really feel about it?" "What is my true core emotion?" "Am I really facing my feelings?" It can be confronting to face ourselves; but, in spite of this, we are responsible for the mirrors reflecting back to us.

There are so many areas to work on. It is best to work on one at a time. We are complicated creatures so it takes time and commitment to alter emotional patterns. These patterns are deeply etched into our souls, so be patient and remember to go easy on yourself.

Now when you do your visuals, support the process by using the emotional component. Feel how you want to feel as if it has just happened. Feel loved to be loved, feel rich to be rich and feel accepted to be accepted. You will have different emotions and areas to work on than me. Work out your own issues and the way you choose to address them. With this work, there is no right or wrong way. It just is.

Be aware that emotions vibrate at certain speeds. Higher energies are love, peace, joy and happiness. If we feel these higher emotions, we will attract the same from other beings. It is the law of attraction.

We are all little energy packages beeping signals to each other. In changing our signals, we change our life.

Accessing Spiritual Dimensions

Choices allow us to expand our consciousness and take us to places where much learning can take place.

Portals

In our reality portals don't exist, but spiritually they do. They have existed since the beginning of time. Portals are gateways placed around the globe, the entry and exit points for energy to flow into our atmosphere. Knowing about them can help us understand how energy can move in and out of our world. If we could see them, they would look like holes in the earth's atmosphere.

Sometimes various portals are open, while at other times they can be closed. There are stories about spiritual battles taking place around these portals. Some people believe that particular beings would like to own them. I have met some psychic souls who have told me that they can astral travel and thereby actively engage in these wars. Everyone needs to make up their own mind regarding these matters. Personally, I am more concerned with working with the new energies on the earthly plane.

I do know that individuals who are skilled at astral travel use the portals to move in and out of the earth plane. I am unsure if this has been part of my reality, but there is much, we still don't know about these occurrences. So I leave it to you to decide.

I do know that at particular times the portals are more open allowing great flows of energy and light to enter our plane. With this increased flow of energy, the vibration of the earth is affected, and it changes the speed of life on earth. Whenever the portals open in this manner and the surges of energy come through, all of us are directly affected. Mostly, we will feel unsettled and ungrounded. Our soul might be able to sense the new energy, while our human side is unaware of these shifts.

If we are open to receiving energy our soul will automatically absorb it, thus changing our vibrational rate. In time this new light will gradually move us up to the next dimension. For now we have mostly been in the third dimension, however, with the influx of higher energies many have moved up into the fourth dimension. Some advanced souls, who were already vibrating at a higher rate, have used the light to move to even higher dimensions.

With the change comes more spiritual access. It is like the heavens open and the lines of communication become better. Everyone is moving up at various rates. Even the heavy ones, full of doubt and intolerance, are being affected by the vibrational shift.

The portals have been recorded in earlier cultures. While they may be a new concept to us, they were acknowledged by several civilizations. People knew of their power and existence in Egypt, Tibet and South America. In the world of science fiction there have been stories of battles being fought over ownership of these gateways. The predominance of movies about these gateways shows us that on some soul level, we all know about them. Often movies expose us to ideas we aren't quite ready to accept as part of our world yet.

There are many hot spots around the world. I am sure there are active portals in these places where enormous energy exchanges are taking place. To me, it seems like the new energy is having a hard time coming through. These portals can become hot spots if there is resistance to peace and advancement. The light brings with it change and not everyone wants change.

When the energy comes in we can make a personal choice, whether to receive the higher vibrations or not. Free will reigns. I always want to move ahead and experience greater enlightenment, so I intend to gather all the energy I can absorb. I believe this intention to receive helps the energy to be absorbed more easily into our energy field.

We are by nature stubborn, and often, resistant beings. Despite this, I feel that just by deciding to be open to the new energies means we will begin to overcome our own blocks.

Once you become aware of the influx of energies you can tap in more easily. Normally, more enlightened souls will sense when the energy comes in and will consciously draw the light in. In my case, an unsettling feeling signals to me that changes are occurring. I usually feel jittery and not as grounded. Occasionally, when new energies are coming in, I can get a "floaty" kind of feeling and can experience more tiredness as my aura struggles to adapt. This comes from the exchange and the general raising of the earth's vibration.

The effect of the new openings

In the next few decades, more portals will be opening. These openings will herald enormous opportunities for mankind. For those who embrace the influx of new energies much growth can be gained, however, for those who resist, life on earth may feel more challenging. We can advantage our growth by receiving these extraordinary energies.

The most obvious change will be in the aura. On a spiritual level, your ascension will be propelled ahead. During these shifts, it will be important to maintain balance in your daily life. This includes eating well, resting, exercising sensibly and having a positive attitude. Vibrating up can put a strain on the human body, and therefore, we need to give the physical body time to catch up. In the energetic world, everything is done with relative ease, whereas our physical body takes time to adjust. Give yourself breaks to rest and deal with any issues that arise.

During this time, your relationships will be directly affected, and you may find your ability to cope with some people can lessen. I noticed that I was getting bored really quickly. I found during this time it was hard to stay focused. You might only be able to maintain shorter connections with those operating at a different vibration to you. It sounds arrogant to say we are bored, but remember it is only a measure of where we are vibrating. What was easy before can become tedious. I discovered that talking about other people and current affairs only kept my interest for short periods of time. I wanted to speak about personal growth, soul work and the real happenings around the world. Some relationships are based on old patterns, so I resign myself to spend a certain amount of time in these more human places. Still, it is hard and somewhat unsatisfying.

I mention this because as you ascend spiritually you will need to be more with others like you. These will eventually be the relationships you will enjoy being in. Your old friends may not want to come along with you on this journey. You will be in a very different place to them energetically.

When you make the shift you may realize that you can't be all of yourself with them because they can't cope. You can go to their areas of interest, but they can't go to yours. If you try to speak about some of your new insights you can lose their interest. Some of your ideas will be totally lost on them.

I thought it was sad to have to couch my words, but I knew they needed me to be "old Wendy," so I did it. Now when I am with them, I choose carefully the areas I talk about. It's more for their comfort than mine because I realize in some ways I speak another language. Regardless, in order to keep true to myself, I let some of my spiritual side manifest when I feel it is necessary.

So how you spend your time, and with whom, will be a decision you will have to make. Hopefully, you will be attracting similar souls into your life. It's wonderful to meet new people. The exchange of ideas always excites me. Remember, some new friends will only choose to go down the path for so long. They can be with you for part, yet not the entire journey.

I write about these issues because it will help explain the way we change. For some reason, we don't realize that when we make energetic changes everything around us changes too. It is the price we pay for ascending.

Opening up to the extra energy coming down will alter your aura dramatically. Your work may change and you may even move house. Be aware of these effects and have faith. As we shift our consciousness, there are so many possibilities for each of us. I focus on my own growth and encourage others to access the new energies. Some people will, and some people won't. Be patient and know that everyone does it when it is right for them. In all things, we have free will on earth.

Our soul knows whenever the portals open. Don't worry about knowing it on a human level. Sometimes, I have been told about a new portal opening by a friend. At these times, I make a conscious effort to release old energies and accept the incoming energies. Still, if you don't get told, don't worry because your aura will be able to access the energy. All of us constantly tap into the universe. With your intention to be part of the vibration ascension, all will be set in place for your growth.

The spiritual world works in mysterious ways. Have faith and all will be delivered in perfect timing for you. In your time and in God's time.

Spiritual frontiers

Most of us have been living in the third dimension. In this dimension, we are defined by time and space. It is a tangible world. Over time the world has been vibrating at a faster rate, and gradually we are moving into the fourth dimension. As we have ascended, so has our personal ability to reach other dimensions. Our minds have also expanded, so we can access more fourth-dimensional concepts.

Of course, there have always been those who naturally lived in the fourth and fifth dimensions before the rest of us caught up. They were the psychics and new thinkers who made startling discoveries. In their time, they were very unlike those around them, and they knew it.

Today it is a bit easier to be different. With the coming in of the next dimension our minds have been opened considerably. There is a new consciousness capable of seeing the bigger picture. While the third-dimensional thinking hangs on, there are enough fourth-dimensional beings to keep the world moving forward. Our minds are expanding at a quickening rate. Soon many will be able to do, what was previously only open to a few. This is especially so in the spiritual realm as many people are finding their own spiritual awakening.

The more we delve and discover worlds without physical boundaries the higher will be our ascension. Thought forms, energies known, but as yet unseen, and telepathic connections all take us closer to the fourth dimension. Work on ascending. Ask to be shown the path for you. For each has their path to walk. Although there are many marching forward to the same Light, each walks an individual road.

It is an exciting time energetically. Work on yourself and assist others to move forward. Once we step into the fourth dimension some will be able to continue into the fifth. Just follow the lighted way knowing that all will be well.

Soul dimensions

I accept that we don't all live in the same dimension. Our physical body may live in this dimension, while our soul can move and reside in other ones. Usually we exist physically in the third dimension. This is a space that humans have invented to define a place that does not really exist. There is no space, but we need to invent it so our lessons can be anchored into some kind of place for our human side.

On a spiritual level space is not necessary. It serves little purpose. We use it here as a stage on which to perform. Space and time are our greatest enemies. We are spiritual beings existing in our heavy armor. The weighty feeling is energetic. The newborns feel it immediately. At birth, their place of peace is gone, and they begin to feel the fear and anger so prevalent on the earth. Earth is heavy and lacks the finesse of the other realms. I consider those who come here to learn or help take on a big challenge. The major difficulty is to do with the denseness, as the vibration is much slower. Consequently, it is hard to be vibrating on a high level and live here.

At this time when the earth is shifting to a higher vibration everything is moving more quickly. We are able to vibrate faster and as our auras become clearer older energies can be released. This serves to lighten the aura and helps us to ascend spiritually. In some ways, this makes it easier to move ahead, but even so, the energetic gap between people continues to exist.

All is speeding up. Everything on the earth is vibrating more quickly. With this increase comes more understanding of how the universe works. Some call it "the quickening." As we move through the dimensions, there is a knowing. People are seeing the connections between things and grasping new concepts with openness, instead of ridicule. As we ascend on an individual level, the group ascends as well.

I see the dimensions overlapping one another. So we can be in the third and fourth at the same time, one overlapping the other. The dimensions are one upon the other, like laying many colored sheets of paper one on top of the other.

Spiritual ascension contains all the dimensions. When you are working on moving up through the dimensions it is important to remember this. You are still a physical body living here, and it is necessary to look after yourself with good food, exercise and rest. You need to operate in the world on a social level as well. Keep grounded because it can be easy to want to be living in the ethers.

You have chosen to be here and live in the third dimension as it moves into the fourth. So while you move up further, don't lose sight of your place in the world. Enjoy the physicality of the earth, including the food, nature and worldly goods. It is okay to embrace being human and the gifts of life. It will help to keep you grounded while you continue to ascend.

Spiritual growth can actually be enhanced by staying in the "real world" as I call it.

Many are here from other galaxies, from other dimensions of knowledge. They have already lived in overlapping dimensions. Although in human form for this life, they really come from a multitude of other places. The world at this time and space contains an eclectic group of entities. Although we are all dressed in the human form, we vibrate very differently. There have always been those from other realms throughout the ages. They brought with them power and knowledge to assist and challenge the world.

Today many beings have chosen to be here at this time to assist in the awakening. As our consciousness vibrates up to the next dimension their very presence on earth helps in the shift. The more souls on earth vibrating higher means the shift can be easier and quicker. The trend toward more spiritual endeavors aids this vibrational growth. Moving a whole world to the next dimension takes much energy and intention. Individuals who are working on their own ascension are shifting it also on a universal level.

You can ask to move up into higher dimensions. Just with your intention Spirit will guide you to the next one. Not only will you be helping your own personal growth, but more importantly, in the world shift. As we move up it becomes easier to connect with other spiritual beings. The gap between us becomes less, so communication is more accessible. Once we learn to vibrate up and down into the various dimensions this connection improves.

It takes much energy to vibrate at a higher level, especially at the start. Keeping your vibration up can be tiring at first, but with practice and over time going in and out of the various dimensions becomes less taxing. There may be times when your physical body is not strong enough to accommodate the higher vibrations. Be aware that you have to give the body time to get used to the increased frequency. For example, I don't try to move up when I am very tired physically or when I am sick or upset. Your body will adjust over time, so be patient. We are a work in progress. Some days you may be able to be higher for a few minutes, another time it could be for weeks. Vibrating higher can stress the body, so be aware of the impact it is having on you and adjust your expectations accordingly.

I have come to realize we are all here to move into the higher dimensions. How and when we do it is totally up to the individual. It is your own personal journey. Never berate yourself or compare yourself to others. It is better to work on your own growth and allow others to do the same. Although we may be all heading to the Light, our paths will be different.

Each of us has a unique soul history. Each of us has come to earth for personal learning. Remember though, we all work within the universal Light.

Through Time and Space

There is no time and space. We are but actors in the world of life. Once we set ourselves free of these constraints, we can travel to all dimensions.

Divine timing

Divine timing is universal time. I know it sounds strange to use the word time when the universe is timeless, but divine timing means something different. On the earthly plane, we are so hung up on time, whereas universally it is not important.

Divine timing refers to the order and sequence of events. It is not strictly about time, but the experiences in time. For example, divine timing may apply to meeting someone and refers to where both people are in their life journey. Although two people may be destined to meet, the timing has to be right for it to occur. Therefore, one may be ready to meet, but the other person is immersed in another relationship. Obviously, it won't happen while one is fully occupied in another relationship. The first person will need to wait until the second one has completed their part in the current relationship. This is divine timing at work.

Divine timing may incorporate several opportunities for the same event. I think this kind of timing is on a cycle, and you get a few tries before the "time" runs out. Maybe a certain job is your destiny. Typically, you may be given a number of chances to obtain it. The same job may come up again in order for you to grasp it if you were unsuccessful initially. It's like being on the merry-go-round, so if you miss it the first time, another chance is given.

In the years before the event happens, the timing was being set up. The doors of divine timing open frequently because Spirit knows what strange beings we can be. I think they factor in our fears and the distractions when presenting us with new chances. Waiting for divine timing to come can be disheartening. It can take decades in our time. For specific discoveries or ideas to come out, other world considerations need to be factored in. The world also has to be ready to deal with new concepts. The greater the shift the concept makes, the bigger the overall effect. Therefore, many things need to be firmly in place for this to occur.

Pushing against divine timing feels frustrating and is fraught with obstacles. Your intention and will may be strong, but everything fails. No matter which way you try to go, it ends up the same, absolutely nowhere. We have all pushed against the timing; it seems like a human trait. Our attitude is if we try long and hard enough it will work. While I was trying to publish my first book, I had firsthand experience of divine timing. I had sent off countless letters to publishers and agents. I was working hard to get my book out there. I wanted to help others. With this in mind I believed that all would be delivered. After countless rejection letters, I received an acceptance letter. I was overjoyed. The lady wanted to publish my self-help book, which dealt with abuse. Unfortunately, before my book could get to the print stage the publishing house dissolved. Unbeknown to me the husband and wife were in an abusive relationship, and the marriage split up. Consequently, the business folded. So did my opportunity for publication. At the time it seemed like a universe joke. Divine timing, it wasn't!

Being aware of the effects of divine timing can help to explain some situations. Not everything is about us. Time after time, it is literally dependent on others and their choices. In some circumstances, others may directly affect our divine timing too.

Divine timing can be a wonderful and annoying aspect of life. I think for it to work smoothly all things have to be in place. I tend to leave things to the angels as they see more, and they are privy to the greater working of the universe.

I believe the loveliest part of divine timing is the flow. With it, everything, you are trying to achieve falls smoothly into position. It is like the sun shines down upon it all. It feels like the door of fortune opens and everything goes off well. That is a sign of the timing being activated because it is right.

Spiritual time gateway

A phenomenon can occur in the spiritual world which I call the "spiritual gateway." It happens when a special outcome is necessary in the spiritual world. You may have already experienced the spiritual gateway, but been unaware of it until now.

Perhaps you are destined to live in a particular place or get a specific job. It is a spiritual necessity for your path and growth and has been set in place before you arrived on earth. This is when the gateway is activated. I first encountered it when we were buying our third house. I knew in my heart that when the house turned up, I would "know" it was the right house. Like everyone, we scoured through the papers and went to numerous open inspections, all to no avail. My husband was getting sick of looking every week and hearing me say that it was not the right house. The whole family was fed up with it. Then one night I had a vivid dream. In the dream, I was shown a house with an outdoor room. I mentioned this to my husband, and he searched the net and saw a home with a similar room to my vision. He dragged me, quite unwillingly, to the inspection. Instantly, I loved the house and knew this was it.

As luck would have it, there were lots of interested buyers. In the afternoon, we put in our bid and waited. An unusual thing happened. Our bid was uncontested and accepted straight away. The seller told me she just knew I had to have the house. As soon as the contract was signed the agent's phone began to ring. People were offering more than we had paid, but it was too late. Later I understood that Spirit had held everyone back until we signed, and only then was it opened up again. The spiritual time gateway had been closed until the outcome was achieved. Once done, the time gateway reopened. If you look back on your life you will find similar instances where the time gateway was temporarily closed until the desired outcome had been achieved.

Time gates are very important on earth because we work in a time sphere. The way others are blocked until we are able to secure the house, job or whatever, is crucial. On a level, everyone knows this happens. In these cases, we say that a person was in the right place at the right time. The reverse is equally true.

There are times when you know subconsciously that you need to do something now, or it will be too late. I believe you can tap into that time gateway being opened and sense when it closes. People will call it a hunch. I am sure it is when your soul is leading the way.

I ask for these time gateways to be opened for others. I then ask for us to be guided to walk through them at the correct time. Being such complex creatures we can easily be distracted or resistant, therefore, asking for help seems like a good idea. Living in a world of time means we need to be aware of the limitations it places on our lives.

There are occasions when we can be given another chance. We may miss the first time a spiritual door opens, but be granted another opportunity. I knew someone who desperately wanted a beautiful little villa. She was unable to sell her first home in time to secure her dream home. In the following months, I suggested she contact the owner again and make an offer. She did and her offer was accepted. So the door can open later if it is meant to be. As humans our part is to recognize the door is opening and be ready to step forward.

They say time waits for no man, but when it comes to the spiritual world all can be made possible.

Magnetic doorways

I discovered our actions can create magnetic doorways. These are openings to another path or movement ahead. Many times on earth our paths can be stalled or blocked. We might find we aren't where we need to be at a particular time, and the door can be blocked by our actions or others.

By and large, opening these magnetic doors needs a physical action, a thrust forward. When I was trying to sell our house, I was told to take something from the new home we had bought and place it in the house to be sold. We had purchased the second property and needed to sell the old one in three weeks in order to avoid bridging finance. I did not question the message and just did it. I bought a set of cushions from our new home and placed them in a prominent position in our old home. The house sold within a day. I was thrilled. To be honest, at the time I was unsure whether I was imagining that my actions had propelled the sale.

Over the years, I have seen one action move another area in the desired direction. One of my sons experienced a similar energetic door opening. He was trying to move into a difficult career. He had done all the required work, but things were not opening for him. One of my psychic friends suggested he began to make other plans and focus on moving ahead regardless. This movement ahead energetically unstuck the original career choice, for by opening one magnetic door, it freed up another.

The mere act of pushing forward regardless can affect everything else. So if you want to move house and are feeling stuck, begin to sort out and pack up some boxes, as these actions will help to propel the movement ahead. It can be hard to know whether we are holding ourselves back or if others are. Instead of dwelling on this, work on opening another door, for by shifting one area other energy doorways can open.

We encounter magnetic doorways every day. They are fundamental to spiritual life and the doors, like our chakras, open and close subtly every moment. I found that the information about magnetic doors was fascinating. Knowing we can move energy around is exciting, as we can be the masters of our destiny. Now I know, if we get held up or stuck, there are various energetic practices we can use.

Remember, the solution may not be directly in front of you. It can be to the side of the problematic boulder. Think laterally and make another physical move and, in doing so, you have a chance of shifting the actual doorway to your dream.

Using energetic wings

You can sometimes move things energetically. I have done it using intention and visualization. I was shown how to put wings on places, people and situations needing help to move ahead. On occasions, in the denseness of earth, the energy can become stagnant and this energy can paralyze certain projects.

I realized the wings could help to move people forward in their endeavors, so the wings were sent to various people. I also sent them to some slow-moving projects to give support on a spiritual level. It can be difficult for some people and projects to take off in the earth's dense energy. The extra energetic wings can lift and lighten these projects and people and thus support the journey forward. Lengthy projects and situations can loop on themselves, almost strangling movement.

Humans are emotional by nature. Disappointment, depression and frustration are slow, constricting energies, and can weigh us down. Over time the load gets too heavy for some to cope with. It is easy to get bogged and before you know it stagnation has set in. Time and again, other people see it before those directly concerned. By adding wings, these emotions can be released, for the wings' lightness counterbalances the heaviness of the situation.

Wings can easily be sent to those nearing death to help them pass, giving them a helping hand in their progress to the other side. These wings, attached from the earth plane, can help Spirit move them on to the next world. The wings do have a different quality to just sending love and light because I believe wings resonate more with the angelic realm.

As inhabitants in this world we alter the energetic flow of Mother Nature, as our energies affect her on a daily level. Places on earth can become heavy with negative energy. We have all driven through suburbs saturated with this type of energy. You can almost feel it being soaked up by the earth and the sky. These areas become stained. You know the shopping centers where it feels awful and after being there for a few minutes you can feel the dankness and all you want to do is leave. Wings can be sent to these places too. Anywhere you feel drawn to send wings is good. You can do much work to support our world with these simple acts.

Remember, that someone who seems unreceptive to healing is not necessarily the one who refuses the wings.

Humans will often shut down this kind of work, but be willing and able to receive help on a soul level. You can never anticipate the decision their soul will make. Instinctively, our soul knows when we need help, even if our human doesn't get it. I believe we are here to do the light work. It will always be the choice of others what they do with the gift that the spiritual world sends.

The wings were an exciting revelation to me. They were easy to pop on, and I could feel the movement when I did it. All light work is an opportunity for a better life. Once I learnt the wing style of energy, I was popping them on everything, people, houses, shops, books and stagnant world situations.

Maybe after a time you can be lucky enough to see the fruits of the work, but most of the time it goes unnoticed. If you are fortunate there can be signs, and you will know that it manifested. Someone tells you about a change, and you know the wings were at work. I always get such a kick of out it when I am told, even though it can take days, months or years.

As in all things, be patient and have faith.

Space as energy

The world is all energy. Generally, we don't think of space as energy, yet space is a form of energy. Some of us need lots of space, while others only use the minimal amount. One of the reasons we need or don't need space relates to the size of our aura. Our auras vary in size, which has nothing to do with our physical size. This size relates directly to the energy contained and held by each individual aura.

Some auras are massive and need plenty of room. Natural leaders have these auras, and so do power hungry egotists. Everyone would know people in their own life who have these large auras. Once they arrive at a function these people fill up a room with their aura spreading out and over everyone else. They become the centre and everyone notices them because their light spreads wide. Normally, these people can wield much power. They can be spiritual, political, business or creative leaders, or they can be the guy living down the road. A bigger aura gives you a unique kind of power, as others recognize this power on an energetic level. In a sense, you stand out.

If we want to influence others we can learn how to expand our aura. There have been great people through the ages who have used this skill for man's greater good. Jesus, Buddha and Gandhi are examples of positive influences. I think in biblical pictures the halos symbolize the energy emanating from their auras. Having a large amount of light means you spread out more than the average person. Even if you are quiet and small, your energetic presence is enormous. Mother Teresa was a fine example.

There have also been people using their large energetic power with disastrous outcomes. Power hungry despots are examples of the darker use of power. On a personal level, you would have encountered similar people at school, work and socially. These people seem larger than life, and others can be in awe of them.

At the other end of the scale are those who have little presence. I call them the invisible ones. Their auras can be shrunken and caved in, so energetically they take up less space. No-one notices them when they arrive, and few listen to them properly when they speak. Universally, with a smaller aura you can be undervalued by society.

People with larger auras may sense the discrepancies and use it to their advantage. They may dismiss these smaller, energetic souls. We have all seen it happening in meetings at work or in social settings. In these situations, the person is treated like their input is not important. I believe how much space we take up in this world has consequences because we are treated in different ways according to this uptake.

It is possible to retract and expand your aura. If you inherently have a large aura, you can make it smaller. You may wonder why you would do that. Well, one reason may be to fit into a particular energetic group. I feel on some level people are intimidated by bigger energy bodies. They won't know what it is about you that makes them feel uneasy, but they know you are not like them.

I learnt how to shrink my aura. My boss was controlling and wanted to be in charge, and I sensed she felt threatened by my presence, even though I did exactly what she wanted. Energetically, I was too large for her. Consequently, before I walked into work, I intentionally pulled my aural energy in and became smaller and less intimidating. I do not advocate doing this procedure too often and for too long. It requires effort to sustain and stresses the aura. However, for short periods of time it is a valuable tool.

You will continue to have the same amount of energy available, but it is compressed. Once the episode is complete, your aura relaxes back into its normal shape. In shamanic cultures, this exercise is called shape shifting. They believe we can shape shift into animal forms, including birds. In my case, I retained my own human identity during the work situation.

We all do a similar thing physically. You see people bending down to talk to smaller children or animals. In this way, they are meeting them at eye level to balance the relationship. Conversely, others may stand over you literally, as a way to maintain control.

If you sense your aura is smaller than you wished you can extend it. Imagine your energy body is larger and puff yourself out to make it bigger. You can extend your energy out to take up more space, and this will give you more power on an energetic level.

I think it is unhealthy to keep your aura retracted. However, expanding the aura over time can be a positive move, for it is good to run more light through your energy body. These days I choose to sit in my own space. I like to respect others need for their space and accommodate them by retracting, if necessary. Be that as it may, it is only when we empower ourselves to own our part of space that we really come into our own.

Everyone shares the same energy. Nevertheless, we all have our own unique energy. We deserve to have an equal share in the world energy and the space. For each are intertwined. Once we realize that space is energy, we can reclaim our power and place in the world.

Embrace your oneness and your uniqueness by using that space in a positive way.

The Spiritual Energy of Money

If we feel the abundance of life, we will never be poor.

Money

Everyone has come to earth to learn their own lessons around money. I feel whether we have money or not makes little difference to our view and our relationship with it. Honestly, in the western world we have few money problems in contrast to third world countries; but when you hear people talk about their money worries you wouldn't think so. Our society is very hung up on money.

Our first lessons with money come from our families. Before we were born our genetic money thoughts were generated from our ancestors and many of us carry these money codes with us. Not all of our money habits come only from mum and dad. I have seen how attitudes to money have skipped generations. So while your daughter is born into a generous family, she can carry the frugal habits of an old great grandmother. With genetic memory, it is all about how our families have thought about money. It is these thought processes that color our money beliefs.

We are all affected by our parents' relationship with money. Not how much they have, but how they view money. During our childhood, we would have absorbed or rejected their attitudes to money. While growing up, I was totally unaware of the influence my parents had on me. My dad was a miser, while my mother spent money whenever she could. He was a very selfish man, who spent money on himself and boasted that he could account for every cent in his bank account. My mother gave generously, and she went without to provide for others. Each parent showed a very contrasting way of using money.

My mum gave you what she always wanted, while dad gave what he did not want to keep. Over time, I came to realize that

I had inadvertently taken on their money issues. To begin to see myself like them was disappointing and confronting. In my mind, I was kind and generous. I had believed I was not into money. That was until I really began to listen to myself. It was a revelation. I noticed I talked constantly about money, the lack of it and how hard it was not to have quite enough. I whined and complained.

I saw the two people inside of me, the generous one and the penny pinching one. Once I began to see myself, I was astounded. By tuning in I could hear old money attitudes I had picked up from my past. Not only were they coming from my parents, I realized I had probably absorbed money traits from the genetic pool before them. Sometimes these traits can jump generations, so don't limit them to your first family. Maybe you are like great grandpa or an old aunt.

Everyone has money issues. It's normal. However, we need to be aware of our family values around money in past and present generations, so that we can make the necessary changes. Remember, what we can't see, we can't change. Once I began to observe my behavior around money, I saw a side of me, I had never seen. Even though I would not call myself a miser, I began to hear my father's words when I dealt with money. It was scary and amazing to find out how unconsciously I had adopted his way of thinking about money.

The money connection is normally the hardest to break because we can be a mixture of being generous and stingy. I noticed that on a soul level I had one money concept, while on a human level I had adopted many of my parents' thoughts concerning money. I had carried my parents' money blocks around in my aura all this time and never even seen it. Naturally, once I was aware I began to release the blocks from my aura. The money thing was monumental for me. It was amazing that I had absorbed their views around money for so long without questioning it.

While letting go of these old patterns around money, I didn't blame my parents or any of my ancestors. I knew I had set up these lessons for my own learning, so I was just glad I had eventually worked it out. These days I choose not to be like that about money, and it feels good to be able finally to see my old ways and let them go.

Personally, I found this information was very powerful. It is a wonderful healing for us for once we embark on this journey around money, as we can come back to our true self. I feel that in letting go of money concerns, we can finally be free.

Money cords

Money is a form of energy; it's an exchange in a physical way. I feel that just like we have a physical body, so too does money. You can touch it. You can hold it. You can give and receive it. Our relationship with money is a direct relationship to giving and receiving and generally how we view ourselves in society is directly related to our money situation. Money can be tied into our place in the world and to a degree, our place in the family.

There is a common belief that money is directly related to love. Consequently, if we did not receive enough love, then we may have the same feeling when it comes to money. Lack of love can translate into people feeling like they lack money too. Ask a rich person if they have enough money and the answer is consistently "no." It is not about the amount of money. It comes down to how much is enough, coupled with a deep-rooted fear of never having enough.

I believe we form cords to money. I had money cords to all the financial situations I had. They were everywhere and it was my way of controlling my life. You might have similar cords. In my case, I had a cord going from my aura with each money activity I did. Visually, it would have looked like strings coming from my aura. The food money, entertainment money, gift money and debt money were all hanging onto their own cord. In our culture people are encouraged to hold onto money in this way. People who live like this are seen as highly organized and in control. I had always admired those who had these attributes.

Sadly, the real reason we hold on to money in this way is due to fear. For it is only by hanging on to all the cords that we feel safe. Underpinning this act is a deep feeling that without holding onto the money, it will slip through our fingers, and we may lose it. So with that in mind we learn to hold on tightly. Even so, while we hold onto the cords, we limit the energy flow. Money can't move while you hang onto it.

As mentioned previously, we can acknowledge these money cords and choose to cut them. It will take much courage to do this visual exercise, as our security and place in the world are directly connected to the cords. When I cut my first cords it felt a bit scary and letting go of the control was a new experience. However, if you can do the cord work, your relationship with money can change. It might not be manifest straight away, but given time the flow of money can begin.

In addition, I suggest you try to see yourself in the river of money and feel the money coming toward you. With this visual in place you are open to receiving abundance. At the same time, you can let go of outdated feelings around money and manifest your own relationship with money.

Past lives and poverty

There are many enlightened souls at this time to assist with the world changes. Most of them have had several spiritual and religious lives. These lives have been in the area of service to others. When I have done card readings for people I have seen their past lives as monks, nuns, healers and shamans. Our past lives remain as part of us. In addition, the values and belief systems aligned to those lives can continue to be active in this present life.

Although these past lives might have been wonderful there can be a negative aspect to all these service lives. It revolves around one's relationship with money. For having lived in countless religious and spiritual vocations, we can develop a strange relationship with money that may create an interesting outcome for us financially. On an unconscious level, we can feel undeserving of having money. During those years of service as monks and nuns we may have made a vow of poverty to which we might still adhere to in this life.

Subsequently, having plenty of money can make us feel uncomfortable. In some weird way, we may feel it makes us less spiritual or enlightened. As a consequence, when we acquire money, guilt is attached and our first instinct is to give it away. If we have lived in poverty and been following the path to enlightenment simultaneously, we could have our money wires crossed. For we may unconsciously believe true enlightenment can only exist in a state of poverty.

This pact with poverty will hinder us now. In this life, we don't have to hold onto the vow of poverty. When we made that vow it was made with deep conviction. It was right for that life. However, it may not be right for now. After several life times being a nun or monk these old ways of thinking can become embedded in our aura. Part of changing our relationship with money is changing our thinking.

Books advocate that we see money coming into our life, and with these intentions all will be well. In theory, it can work, but it can be hard to manifest while we cling onto the vow of poverty. You may face similar issues. Poverty vows and being enlightened do not have to go together. You can have money. You can keep some and give some away if you choose. Alternatively, you can keep all of it. Being rich is not a negative experience.

Once you change your relationship with money your intentions will be free to manifest your own money tree. Unlocking these deep-seated pacts with poverty allowed me to reach a higher state of consciousness as I am no longer shackled by ancient thought patterns. I am free to receive.

Money discs in aura

One morning when I awoke, I was shown an exciting new visualization to do regarding money. My angels showed me little money "discs" in the energy field. Everyone has them. They hang in the aura like little Christmas lights. I was intrigued.

Some are from past lives, while others are in this life. I had always been interested in why some people are money magnets, and others aren't. I realized for some souls poverty or wealth was a karmic lesson. They had chosen to experience the various aspects of money. I knew I had chosen many spiritual lives, and in those times I was taken care of by the church or lived a meager existence. I was fine with that. Then it dawned on me that by living in poverty for all of those lives meant my money discs were not activated. Consequently, in my present

Spiritual Answers to Guide Your Life

life I was walking around with my money discs unlit. I realized I may have fewer discs in my actual aura than other people.

People who are money magnets have lots of discs, and they are all switched on all the time. Money comes toward them, and the discs magnetically grab it. You know the people I am talking about. They remark they don't know how money comes so easily to them. When I checked them psychically, they were like a flaming Christmas tree. When I checked other poorer people their lights were out or sparse and dim. It was then I decided, unless it was karmic, I could activate my discs.

Over the years, I was counting up stray money before I left the house to do food shopping. I seemed to be in a permanent state of never quite having enough. It was frustrating. I did not want more money in a greedy way, only an increase in flow, so I could relax. I had done the visual of being in a river of money and was becoming disillusioned by my lack of flowing cash. There I was in the river with all the cash surrounding me, fishing in a sea of money and catching nothing. However, the realization of the money discs changed everything. Of course, I could not catch much when my money magnets were not activated. Over the next few days, I lit all my past life and present life money discs. To support the process, I asked for spiritual help to bring more discs in.

I had some very financially challenged friends, so I sent spiritual help to them too. In all the cases, I could see psychically they had hardly any lit money discs.

These discs are magnetic, and as such they should draw money to you. Money is really an energetic exchange. Therefore, with all your lights on the universe will be able to help you.

While exploring the amount of money discs in people's auras, I observed an interesting situation. In some relationships, there was a large disparity between the amounts of money discs each partner had. I saw if one partner had lots of lit discs, the other one had hardly any. Obviously, there was an attraction with those who had money attracting ability and those who had none. In our society, we use the term "gold-digger" to explain the poorer one. I remember my husband and I both joking around about this very disparity. We married very soon after meeting. Our little joke went like this. I would say that I thought he had the money. He in turn would say that he thought I had the money. Of course, we both knew exactly how much money each partner brought to the table. It was pretty even. In our case, both of us were running with few money discs. We both instinctively knew our partnership was not like the ones mentioned before, for to have more money, a deficient partner should probably choose a money magnet.

Once you look around at the friends and partnerships in your world, you will begin to see the attraction working. One attracts money and the one doesn't. Rather than find a money magnet, be one yourself. Help to activate your own discs. In love and good faith, send light to other's money discs.

All the work we do spiritually is held in time and space. If, for example, the person has a karmic lesson around money in this life, the light discs we send can be held and used in another life. If we have a karmic life around money, the work we do now will be activated later. Nothing is ever lost.

What if you can't find any discs in your aura

While I was working on the idea around the money discs I had an interesting call from a friend. She could not find any discs in her aura. I was totally perplexed. How could this be? It was then I was made aware of the importance of intention when we do work on the discs. Spirit told me the discs were

Spiritual Answers to Guide Your Life

of a spiritual nature. They were not human discs. In fact, you had to be coming from the right space, a spiritual space, to activate them. The right place meant asking for these discs to be activated as part of our spiritual journey. If we wished for a quick fix for our human wants and desires they could not be lit, therefore, trying to find them from a human perspective was useless. Even so, when we wish to use the discs in a spiritual way, we would easily find them with our spiritual eyes.

I believe if we have forsaken Spirit and our true spiritual path, we may be blind to the money discs. For by moving away from our greatest purpose, we can't access them. Many light workers have stopped doing the real work. Disillusioned with the long wait, they have stopped working as light workers and moved into mainstream employment. Now their focus is more in the human world. The path can be hard and at times, frustrating. Hopefully, in time, those who have hung in there will easily be able to switch on their discs.

Timing also comes into the equation. Spirit will know when the time is right for us. It will be when we are coming from the place of love and the spiritual heart. Everyone is on individual levels, so trust you will be guided. If you can't find the discs, and you are genuinely doing the work, be patient. All comes to those who wait. You can't demand Spirit give you this or that. It does not work like that because control and demand are a human construct. Whenever we embark on spiritual activities, we can only do so when our energy is aligned. Work toward becoming more connected to your guides and wait for the right time.

The discs are there. In time, I hope we are all in the right place for us to activate them. Although I have been given this information to share, there are few who will be able to access the money discs. It does not mean we are not worthy; it is all part of the bigger plan. I hope if you are reading this section you are one of those who can benefit from this information. If not, work on ascending, be patient and all will be revealed.

In Conclusion

Remember to hold your God's hand
as you step into the future.

The spiritual world is vast and full of amazing concepts for us to discover. Now that you have read the book you must come to your own conclusions about the truths you wish to hold. Therefore, use the information that benefits you and keep the rest tucked away for later. I believe we can access what we need when it is the right time for our souls to do so. I noticed that each time I read the book, I gained new insights. Maybe it will be the same for you.

Book one is only the beginning of the journey. In my second book called "Spiritual Answers for Health and Happiness" I explain the workings of the aura and give detailed explanations about the energetic cords we form in life. Being happy corresponds to feeling well, so I have written extensively on all aspects of pain and the release work, we can do to heal ourselves.

"Spiritual Answers for Working as a Healing Channel" is my third book in which I describe the effects various energies can have on our aura and the healing lights available to us. I wrote a number of sections, specifically for those people directly involved in the healing arts. There is a comprehensive chapter outlining the realities of working as a healing channel and positive strategies to use when dealing with clients. The negative aspects of psychic work, including psychic attack and psychic bullies, are included. I discuss other forms of healing and how to use the pendulum in spiritual work.

In a future book, I have been guided to explore our relationships from a spiritual perspective. It will cover how we relate to our lovers, family, friends and foes. I am hoping to write about the most important relationship, the one we have with ourselves.

In time, more will be revealed to us as other teachers come forward and speak their truths. I suppose that is the wondrous part of life on earth. For as we all expand our spiritual consciousness, peace, love and understanding can be ours. It is with peace and love in our hearts that we create spiritual harmony within ourselves, and through these actions, heal ourselves and the world.

Keep working on yourself and, in doing so, you will discover the miracles the spiritual life can bring. I hope, like me the journey brings you "home."

Lastly, I send blessings and love to your heart and life. May you find love, peace, healing and happiness.

With love,
Wendy x

After an electrical accident, Wendy Edwards' life changed from teacher to healer. While living in Australia, she has worked on hundreds of people using her newly found healing and channeling gift. As part of her sacred contract she was guided to write these books and share the wisdom from above.

www.ingramcontent.com/pod-product-compliance
Lightning Source LLC
Chambersburg PA
CBHW032111090426
42743CB00007B/317